COMEDY IS NO JOKE!

The Stand-up Comic's Guide to Success

Vinayak Pal
Co-Producer of the Wicked Funny Show

Comedy Is No Joke! The Stand-up Comic's Guide to Success

Copyright © 2018 by Vinayak Pal

ISBN-13: 978-1986388740
ISBN-10: 1986388743

No part of this publication may be reproduced, stored in a retrieval system or transmitted in any form or by any means, electronic, mechanical, photocopying, recording, scanning or otherwise.

All rights reserved, including the right to reproduce this book or portions thereof in any form whatsoever.

Published by:
10-10-10 Publishing
Richmond Hill, Ontario
CANADA

First 10-10-10 Publishing paperback edition March of 2018

Contents

Dedication	v
Foreword	vii
Acknowledgements	ix
Chapter 1: Starting Out	1
Chapter 2: The Next Steps	13
Chapter 3: Your Own Show	21
Chapter 4: Getting the Network	31
Chapter 5: Two Birds One Stone	39
Chapter 6: Promotion	47
Chapter 7: Loyal Fan Base	55
Chapter 8: Material and Writing	61
Chapter 9: Performance and Polishing	69
Chapter 10: Becoming Good vs Becoming Big	79

*I dedicate this book to my mother,
who worked extremely hard to raise my brother and me.*

*I also dedicate this book to the late George Carlin for all he did
in the comedy industry, with his witty humor and hilarious sets.*

Foreword

Comedy Is No Joke! The Stand-up Comic's Guide to Success by Vinayak Pal is a book filled with useful information about the stand-up comedy industry, and what steps to take that would benefit you and your comedy. Vinayak finds a witty way to make use of his life experiences to illustrate many of his tips, and they are hilarious. I was laughing while reading every chapter! If you are a stand-up comic or booker, I highly recommend this book. If you who aren't, you should read it anyway. It's a perfect read if you just want a laugh.

Vinayak is a charismatic and funny guy. He always finds a way to bring energy to whichever group he's a part of, and I love hearing his jokes. The impressions he uses in his stand-up sets are hilarious. The first time I watched Vinayak perform a stand-up set, I laughed until my stomach hurt. I can't wait till he gets his first Netflix special! When I heard he was writing this book, I couldn't wait to read it. I can honestly say he surpassed my expectations.

He always finds ways to keep me entertained with his stories about stand-up. I love hearing his detailed and hilarious stories of *Wicked Funny*, the shows he's performed, and his work with the Boston Comedy Festival. I am sure you will be seeing him performing all around the globe soon. The bragging rights I will have when I see Vinayak perform on TV will make me more famous. My peers will be envious when they learn I wrote the foreword for the comedic star, Vinayak Pal!

This book is a must read, and I highly recommend it. Don't pass up the chance, because you might find yourself writing and performing great jokes after this. You don't want to miss out on this amazing opportunity to learn about comedy and laugh while you are doing it!

Raymond Aaron
New York Times Bestselling Author

Acknowledgements

The first person I need to thank is more than a person to me. My ma, **Pinki Sinha**, deserves all the thanks in the world. She raised Trishul and me alone, and provided the best education possible. She worked day and night to make me happy, and she invested so much in both her kids, to watch them succeed. I love you ma, and thank you for everything. I couldn't have accomplished anything without you.

I want to thank the rest of my family too, for everything they've done, especially for putting up with my pranks. My brother, **Trishul Pal**, deserves a lot of thanks for enduring the fights we went through. It was like WWE in our house, but our fights weren't fake. My uncle and aunt, **Sanjay Sinha** and **Aparajita Biswas**, took me to different places in India, and I can't thank them enough for immersing me in the culture. I have to thank my cousin, **Chayanika Sinha**, for keeping it secret that I taught her a bunch of English curse words. And lastly, I would like to thank my dida (grandma), **Suvra Sinha**, for loving me, taking care of me, and feeding me the best Indian food in the world.

I would like to thank my girlfriend, **Emma Aaron**, for being the best girlfriend in the world. I cherish all the love we share, and I always find myself reminiscing about the adventures we have been on. She's a driving force that makes my life feel so ecstatic, and I can't wait to see what the future has in store for us. One of the best things about her is her smile because, whenever I look at it, I can see all the beauty in the world. I wouldn't be where I am today without Emma.

I need to thank **Raymond Aaron** for writing my foreword and for publishing my book. He's been a great mentor, and I have learned many life-changing things from him. He has helped me through many difficulties in life, and I'm glad to know such a great guy like him. If you want to succeed in life, then Raymond is the perfect person to learn from.

Much of my gratitude goes out to **Barbara Powers** for guiding me while I was writing this book. She helped me a lot, and I wouldn't have been able to do any of this without her.

Comedy Is No Joke!

Thank you to **Lisa Jansen**, my girlfriend's mom, for trusting me with her daughter and accepting me into her family.

I would like to thank **George Carlin**, **Chris Rock**, **Dave Chappelle**, and **Ellen DeGeneres** for performing amazing comedy, and influencing me to start my career. I want to give a very special thanks to **Russell Peters** because he was the biggest influence on my comedic style and on me. He's a comic I've been looking up to for a while; without his comedy, I wouldn't be here today.

I wouldn't have been able to make it through life without my three closest friends: **Ally Voss,** thank you for being like a sister to me, and for putting up with all my craziness during high school. If she weren't there to keep me in check, who knows how much more trouble I would have been in. **Ciel Yukami,** thanks for all the late night talks and the advice to help me get through parts of high school. I can't forget the guy who I would take a bullet for, **Matthew Ward**. We both have done some wild things together, and thanks for the support through the years!

Much thanks goes to the *Wicked Funny* team. **Daniyal Chawla** is the best co-producer I could ask for. Together, as a team, we can accomplish anything. He has helped me make a great show, and I appreciate everything he does. **Chris Rodriguez**, our DJ, thanks for creating amazing playlists to play at the show. **Justin Scott**, the design specialist, for creating amazing posters for the show's promotion. I also want to thank him for taking the portrait you see on the back of my book. I want to thank **Declan Berkeley** and **Jonah Kaplan**, our video team, for being two of the best filmmakers, and for making good quality films for the show. Thank you **Joshua Hamlin** for helping me reserve the venue for out shows. I would also like to thank the professionals who have headlined *Wicked Funny*: **Drew Dunn**, **Usama Siddiquee**, **Towanda Gona**, **Hedi McLaughlin**, **Carolyn Plummer**, **Sam Ike**, **Brian Higginbottom**, and **Thiago Lima**.

I want to thank my high school graduating class. I know I already thanked **Ally Voss**, but once isn't enough for all the times she has helped me grow as a person. I can't wait for when she opens her own bakery because all the baked goods are going to be so delicious. **Alex**

Acknowledgements

Chang, we are homies till the end. I can count on him for everything, and I am glad I have him as a friend who is basically family. **Leo Wang**, out of all the people in our class, he has roasted me more than everyone combined. He's helped me get thick skin, and also made me laugh countless times. He would be an essential part of the roast team for when I get roasted. **Steven Jin:** he's my brother from another mother. I could tell him something, and I know he would understand where I was coming from. We've been through similar lives, and I can't wait till he takes over the hospitality industry. **Kenny Melin**, he's probably one of the most interesting guys I've ever met. I want him at every single one of my comedy shows because his laugh is so contagious. He's one of my best friends, and I can't wait to perform the bits I have about him. **Yuh Hung,** I love that his name is "Yuh" because it makes conversations so interesting. He has probably said the edgiest stuff to me during my time in Delphi. I probably said edgy stuff back to him. It was great having such a chill friendship with Yuh, and I can't wait to see how much he accomplishes in the computer industry. **Penda Osborne,** she's like a sister to me, and she also helped me get out of trouble a lot. We might not agree on everything, but it's good to know she has my back when I need it. I'm so happy she's in Boston too because it's good to have close friends around. **Michael Clarizio,** he's one crazy guy. I thought I was crazy until I met him. I know he's going to accomplish great things. **Alejandro Olmos,** I still wish I was as handsome as him, and I think my mom's jealous his parents have a son pursuing medicine. He's an amazing guy, and I couldn't think of anybody else who I would trust with a surgery. **Maxine Anderson**, we didn't talk much, but she's a very nice person. I can tell she's going to do super well in whichever field has the honor of her working in it. **JJ Gonzalez**, he's such a cool guy and with his tenacity he'll create an amazing business. I can't wait to see which type of business he decides to start. All I know is that it will be amazing. **Xane Taufer,** he was always a great guy to talk to about current events, and I was amazed at his pottery skills. **Kaden Morfopoulos,** he's an extremely talented photographer, and those skills will take him to great heights. **Faisal Alkathery,** it was nice joking with him about many aspects of life. He is a funny guy, and I hope he's enjoying medical school. **Ivy Ramos**, she's a kind person, and I hope she's having a fun time at college. **Jason Chen**, he's one of the smartest guys I know, and I am not going to be surprised if he gets the Nobel Prize for chemistry or physics. **Joyee Li**, she's a well-rounded person, and I hope for her success in her chosen career path. **Lila Welles** and **Nikki Miller,** they are an inseparable pair, and the future students learning from either one of them will be very lucky to have great teachers. **Mandy Ma,** she's a very sweet person, and I know life has many great things in store for her. **Michelle Gong,** she's going to do very well in the hospitality industry, and I wish her the best of luck. **Natalia Garcia,** her career in fashion fits her well, and I can't wait to see her first professional fashion show. **Phillip Vianna,** he's a very determined person, and I know he will conquer Wall Street one day. **Pranav Kawatra,** we didn't always get along, but I wish him the best of luck in his conquests to be the first trillionaire and owning his own country. **Ria Xi,** she has many talents and with them, I know she will succeed in whichever career she chooses to pursue. **Samantha Fudens,** she's going to do great in the musical industry, as talent or as an agent. **Sean Cvetkovic,** I always called him Ibrahimovic because he was good at many things, and I wish him the best of luck in his career. **Vivi Liu,** she's going to succeed as a photographer because the photos she has already taken are so mesmerizing. **Alex Lipson,** he's already succeeding in the music industry, and I can't wait to hear all about his endeavors. **Index Yu**, she's also very talented, and I hope she achieves great success in the future. They all helped me grow as a person, and I know we will all succeed in our respective career paths. We are a great and supportive group of friends, and I can't wait to see all of them at one of my shows. I can imagine each one of them heckling me during the show just for the fun of it. It's going to be such a great time.

    I couldn't have learned so much without the opportunities provided by the Boston Comedy Festival. One of my bosses, **Jim McCue**, is an amazing person. I am glad he gave me insight on the comedy industry, and a couple shout outs at his shows. Thank you for

Acknowledgements

everything. My other boss, **Helen McCue**, taught me a lot about work ethic promotion. She helped me improve my planning and organizational skills. Thank you for teaching me so much.

I have to thank my high school, the **Delphian School**, for all the opportunities it gave me. Through the program, I became a more confident, capable, and well-educated person. I want to thank my teachers: **Michelle Platt, Torben Hansen, Amy Marhsall, Paula Horton,** and **Larry Price** A special thanks to the dean, **Kelly Hepburn,** and the headmaster, **Trevor Ott,** for working hard to keep the standards of the school high and perpetuating the fantastic educational environment Delphian provides. Two important staff members deserve a huge thanks, and they are **John Kertchem** and **Mark Siegel.** They were my mentors, and they taught me life changing concepts that have helped me become a better and more competent person.

Delphian wouldn't be complete without the rest of the staff. I want to give thanks to the staff working there during my high school years: **Pris Alabaster, Paige Allard, Sue Bader, Chris** and **Iris Baumgardner, Brenda Bay, Dylan Bennett, Kaellagh Bennett, Melissa Bowling, , Bill** and **Martha Blokzyl, Sachet** and **Steven Brown, Barbara Colaianni, Tony Courtemanche, Grant** and **Kori Curry, Emily Dambrin, Dege** and **Rosemary Didear, Linda Drazkowski, Leeya Eskinazi, Todd Forslund, James** and **Robin Gailunas, Mary** and **Russty Gill, Erin Glenski, John** and **Judi Glenski, Scott** and **Kathie Gregory, Evanie Hamilton Hansen, Kelly** and **Sterling Hepburn, James Horton, Madison Hunter, Rachel Karl, Thomas Keough, Heather** and **John Kertchem, Ineabell Laboy, Jocelyn** and **Tom Larsson, Brandon Lidgard, Charity Livingston** and **Joe Sessions, Sue MacKenzie, Diana** and **Don Marshall, Diego** and **Gail Martinez, Tami McCole, Jeanne McKevitt, Melissa McPhail, Char Miller, Kim Neuhauser, Butch** and **Julie Nosko, Jay Nunley, Kelly Olivares, Corey** and **Rebecca Orthman, Leslie Orthman, April Ott, John** and **Paige Perkins, Bill Perpelitt, Terry Platt, Mary Price, Michael Przybylski** and **Irene Smid, Bridgette Rappoport, Jerry Rip, Johann Rodgers, Eric** and **Nancy Roland, Naty Romero-Ott, Aurora Romero-Phelan, Alan** and **Joelle Rothe, Jeff** and **Trish Rouelle,**

Comedy Is No Joke!

Marty and **Cecily Shaw, Jordan Siegel, Linda Siegel, Linnea** and **Sam Silver, Mayra Swanberg, Carol Thoburn, Adam** and **Alyssa Whitworth, Bruce** and **Marti Wiggins, Marsha Worlock, Tkeisha Wydro, Mari** and **Tom Young.**

There has been this one group of girls that has kept me in check, and most of the time they've succeeded in keeping me out of trouble. I would like to thank *the sisters* because, even though we aren't blood related, you all are like family to me. **Kaitlin Moe**, I can always call her and talk about life. It's so nice to know she is there if I need someone to talk to. It's going to be so awesome when she starts veterinary school. **Ally Voss**, yes I know I thanked her for a third time. Maybe now she'll make me a wedding cake for free when I get married. **Quinn Bennett,** she's one of my favorite sisters. It's not because of how much she has helped me but because of how much trouble she gets into. It's like watching a sitcom but in real life. **Meggi Cyrus,** she has helped me out a lot in my sophomore year, and I can't thank her enough for that. It's going to be so much fun when I visit her in Germany. **Sarah Rountree**, I appreciate her efforts to help me find a girl, but they didn't work. She doesn't have to worry now because I found Emma. **Sarah** and **Juliet Holyfield**, I don't remember which one of them has more sass, but I remember they both show a lot of care to the people close to them. **Lorelei Oman**, we might not agree on many things, but she is a person I'm glad to say is like my sister. **Lindsay Carberry**, after all the blonde jokes, I still don't know how she puts up with me. I know she's going to do great. **Callie Whitworth**, her smile is very radiant, and her charisma attracts many people to her. She's going to do amazing stuff in the future.

I want to thank **Sathya Sai Baba** and **Ma Karunamayi**. Sathya Sai Baba's SSE organization taught me many moral values I hold dear today. It's a family I can always go back to, and I'm happy to say I am a Sai devotee. Ma Karunamayi, thank you for all the help and guidance you have given me. I'm grateful for it all.

I would like to thank **Usha Auntie** for guiding me during my high school years. It helped me make the right decisions, and I'm grateful for all her guidance.

Acknowledgements

I want to thanks **Rafik Mohammed** for creating the website for my book. He was a huge help.

I have to thank the woman who's like my mother in Boston, **Sheila Chapman**. She has always kept tabs on me to make sure I am adapting to the weather and to Boston life. I am grateful for all she's done, and she's a splendid woman to be around.

I have to thank **Abhijit Uncle** and **Pinki Mashi** for being my Bengali family away from home. They always make sure I am eating right and enjoying my time in Boston. I appreciate all the care they give me.

For all the teachers and staff providing me with a great educational foundation at Delphi Campbell, I thank you. Special thanks to **Marcy Green**, **Sid Raspberry**, **Victoria Raiburn**, **Nita Kumar**, **Jessica Robles**, **Beverly Cuellar**, and **Erin Franco**. I have to write a personal message to a certain staff member, **Kelly Chambers**. He was my first father figure in my life. He saw that I didn't have a father, and I was struggling without one. He talked to me and played the role of my dad. I am extremely grateful for all that you have done. Thank you.

I'd like to thank Emerson College, and the staff members who have helped me learn during my time here. Emerson has provided me with many opportunities to learn and gain skills in many fields, and it has helped me improve my comedic ability since I started. I would like to give a special thanks to **President Lee Pelton**, **Bridget Schulz**, **Martie Cook**, **Lu Ann Reeb**, **Brenda Wrigely**, **Matt McMahan**, **Erin Schwall**, **Michael Bent**, **Tara Jackson**, **Mary Kovaleski**, **Lindsay Haber**, **Amy Ansel**, **Tim Douglas**, **Jonathan Satriale**, **Cara Moyer Duncan**, **Elizabeth Avery**, **Beatriz Gonzalez-Flecha**, **Duncan Pollock**, and **Johnny Dunbar**.

My close friends at Emerson, who I haven't already mentioned, deserve a lot of thanks. They have helped me through tough class assignments and life problems. Thank you **Josh Gorman**, **Antonio Camasimie**, **Grant Rosado**, **Hardik Pahwa**, **Francis De Leon**, **Omar Ahmed**, **Bethelly Jean-Louis**, **Cole Magnacca**, **Ryan Bellerose**, **Max Schwalbach**, **Jackson Damon**, **James Pandolfo**, **Rupa Palla**, **Josh Whiting**, **Matt Connolly (the lumberjack)**, **Joris Pijpers**, **Marcus Cepeda**, and **Jack Cunningham**.

I have to thank **Seth Meyers**. In middle school, I would stay up late just to watch him do the weekend update on SNL, and now I enjoy his job of hosting *Late Night with Seth Meyers*.

I would like to thank the ***Daily Show with Trevor Noah,*** for what they do to contribute to comedy and current events. **Trevor Noah** is an amazing person, and he is a very funny comedian. I can't stop laughing while I'm watching one of the show's episodes.

I would like to thank **Team Coco**, for all their works and for putting together *Conan*. The comedic touch of **Conan O'Brien** always amuses me, and I can always watch the show to cheer me up when I'm feeling down.

John Oliver, and all the contributors to ***The Last Week Tonight with John Oliver,*** deserve thanks for all they do. It's an amazing show, and I love how John delivers the news. It's extremely funny, and we need more of it.

I would like to thank **Kabir Singh** and **Ezekiel Echevarria** for helping me get opportunities in the stand-up industry. I appreciate everything you have done.

I want to thank some local Boston comics who helped me when I started out. The host of the Hideout Open Mic, in Faneuil Hall, **Hedi McLaughlin**, who has helped me make my way around the open mic circuit. The man with the greatest laugh in Boston, **Shyam Subramanian,** for laughing at all my Indian jokes, and for giving me tips on comedy. Finally, I want to thank **Miguel Perez,** for introducing me to more open mics and for giving me suggestions on my comedy sets.

My time at the **New York Film Academy's** acting camp was one I can never forget. I can't thank the program enough for all it taught me. A special thanks to **Craig Fox** for answering my questions on the comedy industry, and for helping me get started. I have to thank one of my greatest friends I made during the camp, **Abel Haffner**, who is one of the most talented actors I know. Our whole squad from that camp was so amazing and friendly. The other goofball of the squad was **Max Raboin**, and I would like to thank him for supporting my comedy, and me, at the time. The ladies' man was **Francious Boers**,

Acknowledgements

and he deserves thanks for helping me become a romantic; and the ladies, **Sidney White, Ines Asserson,** and **Belle Wiener,** for telling me what not to do when I'm trying to get a girl's attention. The nice one of the group, **Sean Bailey,** I thank her for cooking all those meals with Abel, and for laughing at my Jewish jokes.

My team at the **Global Young Leaders Conference** was a memorable one. I want to thank all the staff members who made it happen, and I give a special thanks to my group leader, **Courtney Lange.** My group was full of amazing people who I want to thank for the support they've given me. It was called the China group, and the members were **Alexandra Rizou, Amanda Romanzini, Angela Rossi, Caroline Kay, Cobo Cabarrus, Delmont Ruiz, Fergus Lupton, Gemma Shaw, Hujar Shehata, Addison Schlatter, Agustina Lugea, Isabella Aboud, Kabir Sacranie, Katherine Hamel-Smith, Louie Zhao, Osbourne Munyambu,** and **Wendy Liang**. There are three special members of the group I want to give a special thanks to. The first person is my roommate at the conference, **Juan Sanchez,** who was able to raise my tolerance level throughout the event. The second is **Janita Himson,** for making GYLC fun, and for creating a little rivalry between us. The third and final person is **Sage Coates-Farley,** for making the conference special, and for making sure I didn't do anything too crazy during the conference.

I have to thank some of my friends from GYLC, who weren't in my group, for making the experience fun and hilarious. They are **Alezeh Mumtaz, Aziz Abdullah, Deanne Diego, Clarissa Fernandes, Sarah Sequeira, Hamzah Al Shahwan, Hasan Kalla, Muhammad Amir, Neha Malcom, Wajih Jaroudi (the camel), John Metz, Chris Varone,** and **Jonathan Pereira.**

I want to thank the **Delphian varsity soccer team** I was a part of for the last two of my high school years. I learned a lot about teamwork, and I grew as a person through our seasons. I loved singing *I Want It That Way,* after winning games. A special thanks to coaches, **Duncan Dimanche** and **Lukas Ott,** for helping me become a better player and teammate.

The **Delphian varsity choir** deserves a big thanks for all the fun I had during our practices and performances. A special thanks to our music instructor, **Craig Baider**, for putting up with my incessant ideas on how to improve the choir, and for giving me the opportunity to choreograph and teach an Indian dance to some of the choir for our performance of *Barso Re*.

My advocacy and work with human rights wouldn't have been evoked without the spirit of **Karla Dana**, and I want to thank her for getting me in the Youth for Human Rights Club at Delphian. I also want to thank **Erica Rodgers** for offering me opportunities to help out with human rights campaigns and other events related to it. I can't forget **Catherine Emrani**, who is the Delphian soccer mom, and one of the staff members who gives the human rights club continuous support.

I want to thank one of my favorite public speakers, **Dr. Eric Thomas**, for the inspirational speeches he has made. They've helped me create my urge for success, and without that, I wouldn't be where I am now.

I want to thank the **Portland Helium Club,** and **Alex Falcone,** for teaching me many things about stand-up. All the lessons were helpful, and they helped me a lot as I was starting out.

Rooster T. Feathers does a great job with its new talent showcase, and I want to thank the club for all the great times I performed there.

I want to thank the **Missionaries of Charity,** and **Art of Living's Light a Lamp Foundation,** for the community service opportunities in India. I learned more about the world I live in, and I was humbled through the work I did through these organizations.

My two favorite bands, **Papa Roach** and **Linkin Park**, helped me, through their music, during some unhappy times, and I want to thank them for that. My favorite songs are still *Last Resort* and *In the End*.

I would like to thank **Ice-T** for calling me a "mothafucka". It boosted my urge to succeed.

My life wouldn't be complete without sports, and I have to thank my favorite teams: the **49ers, Warriors, San Jose Sharks, San Francisco Giants, Manchester United,** and **Real Madrid**. I will always support you all, no matter what, and I am excited for the upcoming seasons!

Acknowledgements

I want to thank my original squad, **Satvik Mojnidar, Shaylan Gokel, Sahil Katrekar, Ankur Gupta, Rishi Raja, Mayank Pandey,** and **Dario Vacca**. You all made my childhood fun and full of adventures.

I want to thank the cooks at Emerson for listening to my unpolished jokes, and for giving me their feedback. There were times when they were laughing out loud, and other times when they weren't. Thank you **Logan Prou, Jose Sebastián Mendoza (Abuelo), Junior Santos, Joel Louis, Marqueas Carter, Jamal Mitchell, Patricia Lavin, Steven Boyd, Alba Duran, Maritza Rubio,** and **Robin C Rodriguez**.

I also have to thank the Emerson security guards for listening to my sets before I would perform them at shows. Thank you **Billy Chu, Denzel Beasley, Jonathan Depina, Naphtalie Dorcius, Kama Lish, Emmanuel Rijo, Madeline Lanzo, Naphtalie Dorcus,** and **Elie Villard**.

Even though I am not pursuing it anymore, I would like to thank all the people I worked with in politics: **Kyle Linhares, Rosy Shatkin, State Senator, Arnie Roblan, State Representative, David Gomberg, Former Representative, Mike Honda, James Chang, Tara Sreekrishnan**, and the **FCNL** organization.

I have to thank my freshman crew from Delphian, the **Torbenation G-Station**. We were a bunch of guys goofing off during class but still got a lot of work done. Thanks **Julian Rivera, Michael Korringa, Skyler Felmier, Alex Chang,** and **Yuh Hung**.

I would like to thank the Center of Spiritual Life at Emerson for helping me out during stressful times, and for having a positive working environment. Thank you **Kristelle Angelli, Brian Indrielle,** and **Jake Freedman** for everything. A special thanks to **Harrison Blum** for giving me advice when I talked to him about my problems, and for giving me opportunities to learn things about the world around me.

I want to thank **Dee Kumar, Demetrios Salpoglou, Chris Salpoglou,** and **Wilfredo Miguez,** who have given me opportunities to help support my mom in real estate.

Chapter 1

Starting Out

"Starting your own business isn't just a job; it's a way of life."
– Sir Richard Branson

As you read through this book, you will be learning many of my tips in comedy. I have included a notes section at the back of this book for you to write down the tips you liked and found to be the most beneficial.

When you decide to be a comic, you are planning to be your own boss. As you become more popular, you will be running your own business, and your product is your talent. Comedy is more of a lifestyle than a job because it isn't your normal 9 to 5. I started my comedy adventure when I was 16 years old. I decided to pursue comedy after my interest in politics died off during my high school years. I interned for a couple of political officials in the state of Oregon, and I also lobbied in DC, once. After all that, I realized politics wasn't for me, so I had to choose a different career path.

Being from an Indian background, most of my family wanted me to be an engineer, and my mom wanted me to be a doctor. I had no intention of taking on either of those professions, so I was stuck not knowing what to do with my life. One day I was watching a YouTube video of Russell Peters, and I loved every single joke he delivered. He performed many racial jokes in this video. I was raised around Indians, Asians, and many other cultures and races, so I was able to relate with Russell's jokes. It hit me that I have been doing similar jokes my whole life. I used to joke around about different cultures, and many of my friends and family loved them. With that in mind, I decided comedy was the path I needed to take. My mom was very supportive with this decision, and she gave up on the whole doctor idea.

I didn't know how to start in the industry, so I watched interviews of Chris Rock, Russell Peters, Kevin Hart, and Dave Chappelle, narrating their starts in comedy. I learned that open mics were the first thing to do, but I didn't know where any were. I went to a boarding school on a hill in the middle of nowhere for high school, which was a huge barrier for attending open mics. I made the best of my time by hosting school talent shows and recording videos of my performances. In August of one summer, I met a New York based comic named Craig Fox. He gave me some good information about starting in the scene, and tips with open mics and shows.

After that summer, I was starting my senior year of high school, and I was able to get transportation to participate in the Portland Helium Club's stand-up workshop, taught by a comic named Alex Falcone. This workshop helped develop my observational skills, find material, and enhance my performance skills. I truly loved it. Later on, I received my acceptance letter to Emerson College's Comedic Arts program. Emerson, being in the heart of Boston, was close to many train stops (called the T), so I had a means of transportation to help me get to open mics. I found out there was a website, listing most of the mics in the area, called Unscenecomedy.com, and I began attending mics.

Before arriving at Emerson, I was in the Bay Area, living with my mom. I love reminiscing about the first time I performed on a stage there. It was at Rooster T. Feathers' new talent showcase. I was allowed in because I was a performer, and the club had special policies for performers between 18–20 years of age. I invited many of my friends to come over and watch—at least the friends who were over 21. That meant my old teachers from middle school, and my mom and her friends. It was a fun time. When I stepped into the club, I could feel the energy from all the lights and lively music around me. Rooster T. Feathers does a great job with their showcases. I had a blast, and I nailed my set. All my teachers had a blast, and my mom and her friends finally concluded that it was a good idea I wasn't pursuing medicine.

Performing jokes in front of my mom was a little awkward, but I took that as an advantage. I had one joke in my set, which was very graphic. The punchline was, "She saw a brown, hairy testicle." I saw my mom's face when I said it. She couldn't believe what just happened. I could imagine the thoughts going through her head, "How did he turn out this way? He used to be such a pure Hindu. And now, he's acting like a beef eater." The punchline did land, but I wanted to get more laughs out of it. I continued after, and said, "I am sorry you had to hear that ma." The whole crowd was roaring with laughter.

Performing at mics in Boston is completely different than performing at Rooster T's showcase in the Bay. I was performing in front of total strangers, and it felt weird the first time I did. When you arrive at mics, you should network as much as you can with the local comics and the host. This will help break the discomfort of not knowing anyone. Some new comics don't really care about that, and they can get on stage and perform phenomenally. That's awesome if you are one of those comics, but if you aren't, talk to the comics at the mic and get familiarized with the group. These connections will help you a lot. Trust me on this because you never know who will go where in this industry. Also, if you are in a hurry because of other obligations, but you want to get one mic in that night, you will want a friend to write your name on the mic list to get an early spot. A lot of mics have a list you write your name down on, and most of the time, a host would announce the comics from top to bottom. Something to ask local comics about is where other mics are located because they will tell you the good ones and the not so fun ones. It's good to attend as many mics as you can in a week.

Find out about comedy Facebook pages so you can join and receive information about new mics or other mics around town. The great advantage about these Facebook pages is that they notify you of the upcoming comedy events, or if a booker needs an additional performer for their act.

Make friends with hosts because they will help you a lot. They decide when you get on at a mic, and if you are good friends with them, then they might let you get on early. They are also a great resource for finding out about how to start a mic, what to look for when starting one, and where the good mics are. How should you treat hosts? This was a question I had on my mind whenever I went to open mics. I asked a couple hosts that question, and most said something along these lines, "Treat me like a human being. Just don't be a jerk, and keep coming to the mics." I suggest you don't try to talk to the host for super long. They have a lot to do, and they want to talk to other comics as well. You aren't the only comic at the venue, so don't be selfish. But, if you have an aching question, ask it. There's no harm in that, but don't try to take all the host's time.

Hosts have duties to do before the mic, so keep that in mind. They need to setup the microphone and the mic stand, and they need to get the list in order. I have one strategy to make a good impression at mics with the hosts, and that's offering my help at mics. Sometimes hosts would tell me, "No, but thanks man," and other times, "Thanks! Yeah, sure, how about helping me out with this?" Be someone the host can rely on and think, "He's super reliable." One great way to help out the host is buying food at their venue. Most mics are at bars and restaurants. It's pretty rare to see one not at a venue that's serving food. The reason why these mics are surviving throughout the years is because the venue owners believe the food comics buy would drive up profits. You want to be a part of the group that keeps the mics alive, and buying food is honestly one of the best ways to help with that.

Remember, the hosts are there to have fun, so if you contribute to them having fun, they're going to like you. Hosts are there because they love performing comedy, and you're there because you love it. There's a similarity there, and that similarity creates a great connection. Of course, be friends with the host, but as you're starting out, don't be super obsessed with talking to the host for information. It's annoying to them if you are trying to talk to them the whole time. In the 3rd grade, I used to nag one of my friends to let me try some of his lunch because his mom cooked some of the best Indian food. He kept telling me "No," because he wanted to enjoy all of it; later, we stopped talking because he found me way too annoying. That same situation can happen with the host if you aren't careful—don't be like the 3rd grade me.

When you're at a mic, pay attention to what's going on. One huge factor that makes a mic fun is if the whole audience is paying attention to the comic performing. No one has a fun time when the whole audience is on their phone checking sports updates, or what their old high school friends are up to on Facebook. Also, if a mic is known for being a bad venue, then it starts to get a bad reputation amongst comics. When that happens, comics lose an incentive to participate at those mics. Help the mic out by paying attention and giving other comics support. Open mics are a place for comics to feel supported and where they can feel comfortable trying new material.

I commend a comic who did well at a mic. It gives a supportive vibe that I would like in return, and it's something you should help create too. If a comic doesn't do so well, please don't tell them immediately. Unless you are known for being a super honest person, or a comic asks for honest feedback, it's not a good to tell a comic how bad a job he did. Comics would already know that, since they just performed on a stage with a light flashing on them and no one laughing at their jokes. You don't need to remind them. Most mics don't have a lot of stellar material being performed. They aren't professional shows, in which a comic has been polishing his material for months or years. Be aware of all that, and you can help the mics you attend be fun and supportive.

You are going to be at a bar many times throughout your comedy career. Always treat your bartender with respect. If a bartender complains that a comic at a mic is giving them trouble, then there is a high probability the mic will get into trouble or even close down. Don't be that comic who is a jerk to the bartender, and gets the mic closed. Even before that happens, a bartender could also go the host, and the host might give you a warning or ban you from the mic. Most hosts I have come across always find a way to say, "Tip the bartender," in their beginning act. You should tip them to help keep the bartenders happy.

Tips are the main source of a bartender's income, so keep that in mind.

I always ask bartenders their names, and remember them. It's good to do that since you will be at open mics for a while. To make a good impression, I tell the bartender from time to time, "Hey John! I've been hitting up the mic for a couple months now, and I always see how much work you put in to keeping the bar running smoothly." It helps make a good impact on the bartender, and he will remember you for it. I had a conversation with a bartender once, and I asked him, "How do you like being treated while you work behind the bar?" He told me, "Treat me like a friend. This job has some perks because I can talk to you in a very friendly and real manner, and joke around a little bit more than a waiter could." You wouldn't treat a friend like crap, so don't treat your bartender like crap. They work really hard, so always be nice to them.

In the U.S., the drinking age is 21, so if you're in the States, and under 21, don't order alcohol of any kind. Don't even think about doing it. There are plenty of options other than alcohol. I know a lot of bars that sell chicken wings, burgers, steaks, and even quesadillas. If you order alcohol, and a bartender cards you, then you are completely screwed. I had a conversation with a comic after I nailed a new set I wrote, and she was telling me about the open mic scene. I asked her, "What should a comic under 21 do?" She said, in a very loud voice, emphasizing each word, "If you are under 21, DO NOT buy alcohol. I know, with Boston bars, if they find out you are under, they will kick you out and notify other bars holding open mics, which would lead to your exile from the open mic life." She was saying this so loudly that I thought the bartender might ask me for my ID to make sure I was 21, but thankfully he didn't. I was so scared. Here's a tip: if you are talking to a comic under 21, don't yell at them about what to do as an under-aged comic. It's too much of a risk trying to buy alcohol, so don't take it. If you get caught, you will be hurting a lot more people than yourself. The bar's liquor license would be in jeopardy, and you don't want to be the cause of that.

As I said before, the purpose of open mics is to improve your new material and try new jokes. Learning about your craft in stand-up is formulated through your practice at open mics. They help you decide if you want to add certain characters to your bit, or what words need to be cut/added to keep a good flow with your set. Open mics helped me develop my ma's impersonation in my stand-up. I do a lot of jokes pertaining to my upbringing and how my mom still acts the same way she did back when I was 7. Before the mics, I knew how to do a South Indian accent, which is a lot like how Apu talks in the Simpsons. I know Apu is a controversial character now, but I knew many Indian Uncles and Aunties (Uncle and Auntie are like the words Mr., Mrs., and Miss of the Indian culture). I want to emphasize that I am not saying all Indians talk like Apu. When I was younger, Uncles and Aunties would say things that I found annoying, "Why do you like dinosaurs so much? Go into physics. It will actually help you do something in life." I would imitate them with Apu's accent, and say, "Now that I have heard your complaint, I might fix it. Thank you, come again."

Mics help you figure out what jokes need to be improved. I have heard some comics say that when a joke has gotten many laughs, a comic doesn't need to keep performing it at open mics. That's not true at all. Sure, polishing unrefined material should be a priority for you, but you can find ways of making that hilarious joke even funnier! Also, you can always find new ways of delivering that joke, which could make it funnier than how you used to perform it.

Here's a personal example, demonstrating what I just told you. I perform this joke, and it starts out like this, "I had a friend who has two big front teeth. He was complaining about these teeth one day, and I told him, 'Bro, the problem isn't your two front teeth. The problem is that the rest of your teeth look kind of small.'" The joke continues, "I believe I talk like that because of my ma. When I was younger, I always told Ma, 'All my friends are calling me fat.' She said, 'You're not fat; you just have a big appetite.' Or when I tell her, 'Mom, my friends are calling me stupid,' she would reply, 'You're not stupid. You just want to be a comedian.'" I like this joke a lot, and I use this as one of my openers during my sets. I didn't stop performing it at mics though. As I kept performing it, I thought of a third part to the conversations I had with my ma, "I went to my mom, and said, 'Ma, all my friends are calling me ugly.' She would reply, 'You're not ugly. You just look your father.'" I absolutely love that new ending. My friends love that joke more than the normal audience member because they know my dad left when I was young. That knowledge adds either more comedic affect or less, depending on who is your audience. It's a good goal to have every open mic you go to be amazing. Keep in mind, performing at mics should be a learning experience. If you already knew how to make audiences laugh till they are in tears, you would already be having your own Netflix specials.

At open mics, you should find ways to record your sets so you can listen to them again to find out where you need improvement. I don't always do a video recording of my sets, but it's good if you do. I usually open up my phone's audio recorder and start recording when my name gets announced. I keep it in either a jacket or pants pocket so my phone can get a clear recording. This strategy is perfect to point out where I need help in my sets. It's a great tool and utilize it as much as you can because you're not going to remember your whole set at the mic. Going to mics with friends is fun, and a great thing about it is that they can video record your set. It helps a lot when you are trying to figure out how to improve your movements during your set. If you don't have a friend, then you can set your phone somewhere close by the stage, and have it already recording. I don't always suggest that because you never know when your phone will fall over, but it's one way to get a video recording when you're on your own. Also, you can ask another comic at the mic to record your set. I bet you will find one who is willing. If you are wondering how to set up your phone in time for the recording, just ask the host when you will be going up, and who's before you. Plan everything accordingly to that information.

If you forget to record one of your sets, don't fret about it. There will be many mics throughout the week you can perform at. I always tried to get to at least five a week. I always had many opportunities within those five mics to record and critique myself. I have a personal routine at the end of the week, where I go over my recordings throughout the week, so I can figure out how much I have progressed with my sets.

I still record my sets and send them to other comics I trust to give me their feedback. These comics usually are people I have befriended and have known for a while. They also have been doing comedy longer than I have, and have stellar advice for me. Sometimes their advice totally changes my perception of my set, and it makes it so much better. Don't be scared of other comic's critiques of your set. It's only there to help you, and if you don't like the critiques, just disregard it. You don't need to take into consideration anything you feel doesn't help.

Critique yourself one step at a time. What that means is if you see that there are a couple areas, or even a bunch of areas, you need to improve on, then handle each area individually. When I started doing mics in Boston, I realized my stage presence wasn't good at all. It might have been because I was scared that someone might find out I was under 21. But even if that was the case, I still had to fix this problem. So, for a while, I was only working on being comfortable on stage to improve my stage presence. I'm still working on my stage presence today, even though it has improved phenomenally. You will always see me try to find ways to improve it, at parties and at my comedy show, *Wicked Funny*.

You can always improve your stage presence. I remember talking to a great comic named Butch Escobar, who headlined a Rooster T showcase I performed at. He told me, "Kid, you should always work on stage presence. Screw what anyone else says. Just work on stage presence, and things will be great. Do the same jokes if you need to, but focus on stage presence." I do also focus on other things, but that talk with Butch helped me understand how crucial stage presence is. So, after practicing my stage presence for a while, I started focusing on my writing. I still work on crafting my jokes. One fear I had was performing in front of a rough crowd. Well, at mics, you might run into that occasional drunk, so it would be great practice to handle the drunk once he starts heckling. Reading an audience is an ability you learn through your experiences at mics.

I highly recommend you follow my advice for improving one ability at a time. It helped me out a lot, and it will help you. Before you know it, you will be amazing at so many aspects of stand-up adhering to this dogma. But this will only work if you do a certain amount of mics a week. I suggest you do as many as you can, and you will be excelling before you know it. Keep persevering and showing up to those mics!

When you are done with this chapter, I want you to research on the internet where, when, and how many open mics are around you. After you are done researching, make a plan, fully describing how you will get to those open mics. It will help you be prepared for when you start. There is a list at the end of this chapter, for you to write on and use while researching.

Open mics are only the first step, and I have told you a lot about my experiences and tips for them. You are the one who decides to follow them, but they will help a lot. It's a no-brainer that you don't only perform at open mics, because that's not enough to help you get a name. In the next chapter, I will provide information about what you should do when you think you are ready for the next step. It will help you a lot, and get you a couple steps ahead of the game!

Starting Out

OPEN MIC LIST

Location	Time	Day of Week

Chapter 2

The Next Steps

"Life is a journey. When we stop, things don't go right."
– Pope Francis

You don't want to stop your journey just because you do not know what to do after open mics. As I was starting out, I didn't know what to do after open mics. I still go to them whenever I am trying out a new joke. This chapter provides data for the next step after open mics, which I found out through a lot of questioning and research. I am going to be honest with you, most of the work I put in was completely unnecessary. If I had just talked to the right comics, I would have found it out in an instant. Now, you will be finding it out soon because this book wouldn't be worth anything if I didn't tell you. The problem was that I asked many new local comics questions about the next step. There were probably some comics I never talked to who knew what to do next. That's another reason why you should network all the time, so you can get the answers as soon as possible.

The information I'm about to tell you is not extremely surprising. What to do next, while still attending open mics, is perform in pre-booked shows—"pre-booked" meaning that there is a booker for the show, and the booker gets to decide if you get a spot or not. I personally can't believe that it took me forever to find that out. You need to talk to the right comics to find out where and when the pre-booked shows are. Also, if you find a comic who is friends with the booker, then you have landed a gold mine because that connection can help you get a spot. The first pre-booked show I was offered was through the help of a comic I knew, who was friends with the booker. The comic told me to text the booker through Facebook, and she gave me his name. I texted him about how I knew his friend, and I requested a spot on the show. That is the true story of what I did, and the next thing that happened was the booker texted me, and said, "Oh, hey! Yeah, cool. When are you available?" It's sometimes easier to get on other pre-booked shows. There was this one where I walked into the bar and asked the host if I could have a spot. He went through his calendar and asked me about certain dates, and I got one. It could be that easy.

Some shows aren't so easy. There was one where I was asked to send in a video of me performing, and the booker based his decision on that video. I told you in the previous chapter that you should record your sets. It is easier to get an audio recording, but a booker can't have a sound judgment on your performance with only audio. This is why you should have a couple of video recordings of your performances. You don't want to keep the booker waiting because he'll think you aren't legit.

There's a term used in comedy, called "bringer shows". That means you bring a certain amount of friends to a mic or show, and they pay to watch you. It is fun to have your friends come, but it is kind of a drag asking them to pay for tickets. One plus about bringer shows is they're usually in a nice venue, so they would be great places to film your performances. Just be sure to perform polished material you know has worked plenty of times, so the film turns out well. At open mics, you won't get the best videos since the lighting and many other factors hinder the quality. Whenever I had a friend record my performance, the video wasn't still because my friend's hands would keep shaking. The point is, they aren't YouTube worthy, but they are better than nothing. Personally, I like making a good impression, and having a good quality video does bring about that effect.

A way to get a good video, and learn about stand-up at the same time, is to attend a stand-up comedy workshop. Stand-up clubs around your city probably have opportunities to participate in a stand-up

The Next Steps

workshop. Of course, they do cost money, but they are worth it. At the end of each workshop, there is a graduation performance. Most of these graduation shows are recorded. The greatest thing about these videos is that you will be performing material you've crafted over a couple of weeks, with a professional stand-up comedian! The graduation performance gets you a great video, a great crowd, and a new comedic insight. The video of a workshop would be great to send because of the good quality.

You might ask, "How do I find these workshops?" It's not super hard. All you have to do is type in Google, "stand-up comedy workshops". You will find many results. They are usually in the bigger cities, and if you live in a rural area, you will have to travel a bit. If you are a comic living in a rural area, you are probably already driving to bigger cities so you can participate at the mics. Most mics I know aren't in rural areas, but I think it would be pretty cool to do an open mic in a barnyard. I can imagine a cow mooing in the background the whole time, and people are laughing only at the moos. Anyway, find a workshop close to you, and sign up for it. You will have a lot of fun and learn a lot of great tactics in those workshops. I participated at the Portland Helium Club's 6-week workshop, and if you are in the Oregon area, I highly recommend it.

Pre-booked shows are the perfect opportunity to try out the material you have polished. Since open mics have a tendency to be full of comics, you don't really know how that joke would work on an audience. I am not saying you can't do new material at a pre-booked shows. It's just my personal input. I recommend that you do your polished material because you won't be doing pre-booked shows every single day. There are way more opportunities to do open mics, which are meant for you to explore different types of subject matter and perform newer jokes. Pre-booked shows are also perfect to see what flow your set should have. By "flow" I mean the sequence you perform your jokes in to have the maximum comedic effect. There are rarely any open mics that have non-comic crowds listening to you. I only know a few off the top of my head, in Boston. One of those few consistently has a crowd full of non-comics. Now that I'm thinking about it, it is not even a weekly mic. It's a monthly one. So, cherish the time you have on a pre-booked stage, to work on those polished jokes. Remember, each crowd is going to be different. So, keep performing those jokes because you're not going to get the same crowd at every pre-booked show you do.

I can assure you nothing is better than experience with an actual crowd. It is extremely fun, and you will enjoy every second of it, as long as you put in the right amount of work. If you slack off on stage, the audience will read that, and will reciprocate the same feeling. It won't be a good time. If you are pursuing stand-up, then it is your job to provide a great product. That's the goal I have every time I get on stage. Whenever I performed at Rooster T's showcase, I always had the idea to give the crowd a good night. Sometimes that didn't happen, and afterwards I would figure out how to do better next time. It's a learning experience where you figure out what doesn't work and what does. As you go through it, you will find material that will provide a good time for your audience.

You might be wondering who the right comics are to go to in order to find out everything on pre-booked shows. I wish I knew this data earlier. The first time I found out about a pre-booked show was actually through a website, but that didn't help me much because I didn't know how to get on. I contacted the bar that held the show, and asked, "Who is the booker of this show?" They didn't respond to me for a while—like for 6 months. Ask comics who have been in the open mic scene for a couple of years, and the hosts of mics too. They will get you the right information about pre-booked shows.

There is another way to find out where they are, and this would be extremely beneficial for a new comic. You should go to a professional comedy show, and find a way to talk to either the person putting up the show or the comic performing. Not all professional shows are in a comedy club. You can find many smaller ones, within bars, by going to different websites that list the events happening around your city or neighborhood. I suggest that you attend one of the smaller events since the chances of you meeting a professional comic and having a conversation with him are higher. Make sure the comic is familiar with the scene you perform in. The way you can find that out is by reading his biography, which should be on his website. If you find out the comic started out where you are now, they probably have a good idea of the pre-booked shows in your area. You can create a connection with a professional comic through this way, and you can find out information while doing it.

Let's say you have gotten booked, and now you are at the pre-booked show. How should you treat the host and/or booker? Just treat them like normal people. The host just wants to have fun—like a host of an open mic. There isn't much of a difference. Don't get awkward around the host. Just perform comedy at the show, and talk to the people there about how life has been, or about other things that pop up in regular conversations. This is also a perfect time to network. You will probably find a lot of comics at these shows who do not perform at open mics. It will be a perfect time to see if they know of any other shows for you to perform at, as well as to ask questions about things you don't have answers to from other comics at open mics. Ask the host these questions too. It's not like he's not going to talk to you. They want to network also, and to get to know the people they book. When I said to not be awkward around them, I mean that you should not act like a fan girl meeting their celebrity crush for the first time. The bottom line is, don't be dumbstruck. If a cat has your tongue, the most probable thing that will happen is the host might poke fun at you during his opening act. I've seen that happen before, and I don't want you to be the joke of the act, if you're uncomfortable with that. There are people who don't care if they get made fun of during a bit, but I still advise those people not to act dumbstruck in front of a host—it's a bad first impression.

A tip I have for comics who like to be efficient—which should be you—is to figure out if there are any open mics close to the location of the pre-booked show. If there are any, then I urge you to perform at the open mic first, and then go to the pre-booked show. This will help you get in a couple of minutes before actually doing a show for a real audience. You should do this because there is no reason why you wouldn't want to be efficient with your comedy. Efficiency is a good quality to have because it will help you in every single part of your life. Making one part of your life more efficient will also directly affect how much time you can put into comedy. For example, I found an easier and more efficient way of completing my homework, which in turn helped me allocate more time to write jokes and to organize my comedy show. This might not be fully related to pre-booked shows, but take that tip I just told you. It will help you a lot, and you will be prepared for your pre-booked show. It's better than repeating your bit to your mirror in your bathroom.

Asking the booker to book you again, on a show, isn't an uncommon thing. Don't be shy about it and like I said, don't be awkward. Bookers, for these shows, know that you want to have more stage time. You have to remember that these guys are comics too. If you come across a really nice booker—I've had the luck of coming across many—they will help you out. Ask the booker, "Can I get another spot sometime?" Or ask a question similar to that one; if he likes you, he'll probably say, "Sure. What dates are you available?" It is not a hard thing to do at all. One thing about this business is that you need to have a high confront. By confront I mean the ability to handle something comfortably. You can probably imagine a time where you felt a little uncomfortable, or embarrassed or nervous, for asking a favor from somebody. You're going to need favors from other comics, so you will need to be able to confront talking to other people. Confront affects various aspects of comedy. You need a certain amount of confront in order to perform on a stage comfortably. Your audience will sense if you are uncomfortable, and they will probably not enjoy your performance. You will observe this at open mics, and when you watch other comics.

What can you do to help the host? Here's another reminder. Usually, you will be going to a bar that provides the venue the pre-booked show is held at. A great way of helping out the host, like at an open mic, is to buy food, or drink at the bar. One of the major reasons for the bar owner's decision to let a pre-booked show take place is because he thinks profits will rise with the amount of food being bought. Be a comic who helps keep the pre-booked show alive. That's probably one of the biggest ways you can contribute. That isn't the only way to help out. You can probably think of many other small ways to do so, which is great, and it will take you a couple steps ahead in the making good impressions department. What I want you to do, after finishing this chapter, is right down a list of at least five things you can do to help out your host. It could be for an open mic host or for a pre-booked show host. The way you can help out either one is very similar.

Continue on to the next chapter because it will go over how I created my own show at Emerson College, *Wicked Funny*. It's not a TV show, e.g. SNL, but a live stand-up that I put up every month with my co-producer. I will be going over my recommendations to help your show succeed and keep prospering.

Comedy Is No Joke!

LIST OF HELPFUL ACTIONS

Chapter 3

Your Own Show

*"Stand-up comedy is mine: it's my entity; it's my brand;
I own it. I do it when I want to do it."*
– Kevin Hart

    I love performing stand-up, and I want to make it my brand. When you hear Vinny, or Vinayak, I want people to think, "Oh, he's the funny stand-up." One way I brand myself is by having my own stand-up show, *Wicked Funny*. I enjoy organizing it, and performing as well. It isn't a mic, but I will go over setting up mics in this chapter as well. I use it as a way of branding myself, and a means of networking with the professional headliners I ask to perform in it. It's my favorite part of college.

    Having a show is great because people will come to you and ask you for stage time. This means you are also the booker. As a booker, you start understanding how it feels to be one, and to know exactly how a booker wants to be treated. This is good knowledge to have since bookers get you on shows. As a booker and performer, you have complete control over everything. Don't let people boss you around with your own show. That doesn't mean that you reject advice someone gives you, but just keep in mind you are your own boss.

    A great perk to all of this is that you get to decide how much time you get on stage. So, if you want 15 to 20 minutes, then you can say, "All right, I'm going to get 15 to 20 minutes." That's plenty of time to work on a bunch of new material. There are many advantages when you start your own show, but there is a lot of work needed to create and perpetuate it. One way to keep it alive is by hiring professionals to perform at your shows. I like hiring professional headliners, not only because of the incentive to have a good crowd, but also because it's a great way of networking. In comedy, the idea is if you help someone, then he's going to help you out in the future. A great advantage of hiring professional headliners is that you know they're going to do a pretty good job. So, even if your set isn't super funny, you know they're going to get the audience laughing with their set.

Starting a show isn't the easiest task because you need to find ways to capture a person's interest in order to get them at the show, which means you need an incentive. Be creative with your incentives, and figure out what attracts people to spend time at a comedy show. There are a couple of reasons why an incentive is necessary. One is because you are asking someone to take time out of his or her day to come watch your show. The biggest reason why they would come watch the show is if it is really funny, and/or it has a little bit of a twist in it that other shows in the area don't have. For example, *Wicked Funny* is the only show at Emerson that hires professional headliners to perform. That's how we are different from the other shows at Emerson, and that is our main marketing point. That incentive is the reason why *Wicked Funny* is still a show today. If we were exactly the same as other Emerson comedy shows, then we would cease to exist. There is no point staying in the sea of sameness. You need a brand for your show, and the only way to achieve that is by being unique.

A huge part of getting your show out there is through business techniques, which I will focus on for the rest of this chapter. It's essential to promote your show. If you are in a college, then putting up fliers and posters around campus is tactical. Using social media (Facebook, Instagram, and Snapchat) is another great way of promoting since many people are on their phones. Create Facebook events because many people will share those events with their friends, and you will be getting hordes of people. Emailing is another helpful strategy for promotion. A majority of audience members, in our last *Wicked Funny* show, came because we had been sending out bulk emails. Keep an email list, and use it as much as you need to. Don't over email because you don't want to annoy your fan base, and you also don't want your emails to be categorized as spam. In our emails, we include a nice message about the show, and who is headlining, and attach the poster or posters of our show. You should include all the key information in your email, which is the time, date, location, cost (if any), fun facts about the show, and anything you think is relevant for your recipients to know.

To give you a picture of a good poster design, I will describe what *Wicked Funny's* posters look like. Our posters usually consist of the headliner's headshot, the *Wicked Funny* logo, and all the necessary information about the show. You can find a full-color, ready-to-print example of a poster on notjokebook.com.

What if you don't know how to make a poster on any platform? That is an easy problem to fix. You can learn how to use Photoshop, or some other fancy platform. It will take a little bit of time, but being proficient with any of those platforms is an amazing skill to have, especially in the technology age. Many people can't invest the time to learn Photoshop, so I suggest to you a user-friendly platform, which I use to make posters, called Canva.com. This website is extremely simple. If you are one of those people who want a really nice poster but don't know how to use Photoshop, you still have a couple of options. You can find a family member or friend who uses Photoshop, and ask them for a favor. There is probably at least one person you know who can do this for you. If, somehow, you are the guy who doesn't have a friend proficient in Photoshop, I can only think of one option for you: find someone who sells their Photoshop services, and pay them to make you a poster. Get those posters out there, and promote a lot! It will help you a lot.

Branding is HUGE for a show. I remember when we first put on *Wicked Funny*, it wasn't as great as we planned. We had it at Center Stage, which is a performance venue in the college near our cafeteria. Part of the reason for the lack of success was due to the fact this was our first show, and we didn't have all the marketing and promotion strategies we do now. Also, since Center Stage was by a cafeteria, some of the audience members were there for food and not the comedy. At the end of that show, a guy in charge of another Emerson comedy show came up to me and said, "Hey, you should put your show up at the MPR." The MPR is Emerson's multi-purpose room, and all of Emerson's other stand-up shows take place there. Daniyal and I didn't want to use that venue because we wanted our own area, and we wanted people to know that Center Stage was for *Wicked Funny*. That's a branding strategy.

If you have a location, and people know that it is associated with your show, then that location is related to your brand. That is why we didn't want the MPR because the stand-up that happens there is associated with the other Emerson stand-up shows. A component of your brand is what incentive or incentives you provide with your show. I know I am talking a lot about incentives, but it is really important. When Emersonians hear *Wicked Funny*, they think it's the monthly stand-up show with professional headliners. You want your brand to communicate to people that your show is awesome. When you have put that idea in their head, then you will push out any other show in the area. That is the power of branding, and you want your show at a point where people are telling their friends, "We need to watch this show." Those are the fans you want! They promote your show for free! FREE is everyone's favorite word!

It is a great tactic to figure out marketing strategies and incentives, but all of that is futile if you do not have a venue. In college, it is not hard to find a venue because schools provide areas to put on performances similar to *Wicked Funny's*. What I did was figure out which Emerson faculty member was in charge of Center Stage, and I got in communication with him to learn how I could book it. After that, I started reserving the venue for our shows. It's different outside the college scene. You need to find a venue, like a bar or a coffee shop, which would provide you the necessary accommodations for a mic or a show. Once you find one, create a business proposal to persuade the owner to approve your show. I have said this before in previous chapters, and I'll say it again: the owner needs to believe that the comedy will bring profits to the business. He's in it to make money.

Once the owner grants you approval, you can start executing your marketing strategies. Since you are helping bring profits to that business, you can ask for compensation. Most comics I know, who host mics or pre-booked shows, except for college students (unfortunately that's me), get paid for hosting. Just remember: the more profits you bring in, the more likely the owner will like you and bump up your pay. Do as much as possible to promote the show and venue, and you will be having a great show, and a happy venue owner.

    A show is different than a mic. If you want to host a mic, you still have to promote it to get a good turnout. I have been at mics where there are only 5 people, and they're not super fun. Being at an open mic with 5 people is like watching a game of golf. The comic on stage is the announcer, and the comics watching are usually quiet, like the golf fans. I know a comic who has a Facebook page with 730 followers, and all of his followers are comics. Whenever the mic changes the location, usually because of venue complications, then the comic only has to post the venue on his Facebook page, and he gets a great turn out. Social media is an asset you want to take advantage of. Find out which websites can list your mic, so more people can see that it exists. You don't want your mic to be non-existent in the minds of others, when it has been running for a bit.

    You might be wondering why I have a co-producer. There are many benefits to having one, especially if the two of you can work as a good team. I handle booking headliners, finding Emerson openers, getting the reservations finalized, notifying our video team when to be at the venue, and handling the filming permit. I probably have more tasks, but these are the most important ones. Daniyal is in charge of finishing up our posters, sending out bulk emails, updating our Facebook page, and getting our music playlist finished. He's also behind many of our marketing strategies. We both are industrious and extremely ambitious. We do whatever it takes to keep our show at a high standard, and we always try to find ways to improve the show.

    It's very nice doing only half the work because, with my busy schedule, I don't have time to do everything. The same goes with Daniyal. He is also an extremely busy person, and the work he does is all he can handle. The two of us can rely on each other, and get the job done. If you ever want to co-produce a show with anybody, make sure you can rely on them to get it done. If nothing gets done, then the show will go to ruins. It is funny that neither Daniyal nor I have brought our show to ruins—culturally, we're supposed to be rivals. He's Pakistani, and I am Indian, and usually those two don't get along too well. In theory, a Pakistani and an Indian working together is the worst idea since socks and sandals. But we manage to make things work without fighting over India's Kashmir.

You need to be organized in order to have a show. I cannot emphasize this enough because organization is extremely important. I have a list of all the actions I need to do before every show. This list includes EVERYTHING, and I do not mean that lightly. The actions range from simple emails to getting the permit granting us access to record shows. Because I have a co-producer, we split the work 50/50, and he has a list of all of his tasks too.

My first show was a crazy experience. When I walked to the venue, there was no microphone or mic stand, and it was the job of Center Stage's faculty to provide them. In my mind, I thought, "What did I do to deserve this? Which one of the 130 million Hindu gods did I piss off?" It was probably 15 minutes before the show, and I had to find a microphone and a mic stand. The Center Stage main faculty member was gone because it was way past 5 p.m., so I had to find the students affiliated with him, and persuade them to provide what I wanted. They were able to help me out, and they set it all up 5 minutes before the show. A part of my list of actions is to double-check with Center Stage main faculty members in regards to setting up the appropriate tools needed for *Wicked Funny*.

Like I said before, that first show didn't go so well because Daniyal and I hadn't put our openers through auditions. Those Emerson comics treated the show like a mic, and performed mostly new material. The audience didn't have a fun time, and I was embarrassed. My set didn't go so well either, until the last joke. We didn't set the right mood from the beginning, until the headliner started performing, and our headliner, Drew Dunn, saved us. He is the winner of the 2017

Boston Comedy festival. He was extremely nice, helpful, and funny. I learned a lot from the first show, and all of my experiences dictate that you should add as many actions as you can think of to your list of organization. Double-check whatever you think is necessary to double-check. Trust me; you don't want to have a scenario where there's no microphone and mic stand on the stage 15 minutes before a show.

There was another time where I forgot to notify my video team to attend one of our shows. The team came to the show without their cameras, and I asked them, "Where are the cameras?" One member of the team looked at me perplexed, and said, "What do you mean? You never asked us to record the show. We are just here to chill." This is what I call a Vinny moment. "Vinny" is the name I go by because most Americans don't know how to say Vinayak. A Vinny moment is when I do something really stupid, that I should have known how to prevent. A great example of one would be when I dropped the F-bomb in the middle of a 10th-grade class, and the teacher looked at me as if I was just proven guilty. I looked at the teacher, and I didn't know what to say. After a couple of seconds, I thought it would be logical to say these words, "It wasn't me." It didn't help my case that I was the only person standing, and it's really easy to find my voice in a crowd. I just sat down, and kept reading my biology book. The moral of the story is to keep yourself organized and, whatever you do, don't drop the F-bomb during class. Save that for the stage. Also, take responsibility for the dumb things you do.

To keep your show alive, you need to continuously improve it by adding new aspects to it. Nobody wants to be a part of the same old show, over and over again. There are many ways to improve a show and two big ways are to create new incentives and find new ways to market. One thing I had done was partner with a rap group at Emerson, and in exchange for our show playing their rap music in between acts, they helped us promote amongst their followers and friends. Partnerships are a great step towards building better connections and expanding your show. But be careful because you don't know who will stab you in the back. Make sure you know the person before creating a partnership because you don't want that person to take complete advantage of you. Back on the subject of improving, you can find interactive ways for the audience to participate in the show. That is not in accordance with the stereotypical stand-up comedy show, but if you are aiming for uniqueness, then the idea of being a conventional stand-up show should be out the window. Be as creative as you can because it will help you with your show and your comedy.

After finishing this chapter, I want you to make a list of tasks you think are necessary for running a successful show. There is a list available on the next page for you to write on. After you are finished, go over it a couple times, and see if you can add anything to it. Make sure it is a complete list. After that, keep reading to find out my tips on one of the most important aspects of comedy, and of anything you do: NETWORKING!!! The tips will help you get ahead in any game you play.

Your Own Show

LIST OF TASKS

Chapter 4

Getting the Network

"The richest people in the world look for and build networks; everyone else looks for work."
– Robert Kiyosaki

I network all the time because I believe creating connections with many people can get you to a higher point in life, faster than continuing on your path as a recluse. What does networking mean? It means to exchange information and create relationships with people, groups, or even companies. The purpose of establishing all of these connections is to help one another in the future. I like to think of networking as creating lines of communications with others; so, it's many lines forming a net. The more communication lines you have, the more complete your net is. A real net is used to catch animals, such as fish. The more complete your networking net is, the higher the probability of you catching many opportunities to help you gain recognition and a great reputation.

Creating a strong network in comedy is essential because you do not know where other comics you know will end up. If you search on YouTube interviews of many comedians, you will find a whole lot of them explaining how someone they knew and befriended helped them get a writing job on a late night show, or helped them get a gig in a prominent club. I talked to Zhubin Parang, the head writer of *The Daily Show with Trevor Noah*, after a talk he gave at the Edward M. Kennedy Institute. He was an extremely nice guy, and he told me about networking in the business. He said, "I wouldn't have been hired many years ago if I didn't get the recommendations I did from the current writers at the time." He also said, "Be a nice guy to everybody because it's good for people to remember you as a kind person rather than a jerk." I took Zhubin's tips to heart, and I try my best to be a nice guy whenever I'm talking to people. Admittedly, there have been times when things have gone haywire, and if you get into those situations, the best thing to do is put things past you and re-establish a better communication line with that person. One way to do this, and you have probably done this many times before, is to apologize.

How do you network? That is a question I get from many of my friends because they see me networking all the time. Antonio, a close friend of mine at Emerson, left me for a couple minutes, and I walked into a restaurant. When he came back to find me at this restaurant, I had just met with the restaurant owner and had gotten his card and all his contact information. It is beneficial to have those types of skills, and the way to attain those abilities isn't hard. You should have a charismatic persona, which is my opinion. I know a couple of people who are introverted, and yet they are pretty good at networking. The charisma you emanate is indicative to others of your confidence and drive to accomplish your goals. Think of someone who you've met with a high-level of charisma. What did you think of that person? Did you feel their confidence? Whenever I've talked to someone with that description, the first thing I think of is to become friends with that person.

This might tie into the quality of charisma, but you also need to be ambitious. There is a gray area about the subject of ambition, from my observations. Some people do not like interacting with others who are too ambitious. It's a fact, and I've noticed it with people I try to interact with. They have a couple conversations with me, and they think I'm crazy. I know many others who are attracted to ambition, and we'll stick with you because of your urge to achieve your goals. The way I determine whether to show my ambition to someone is by the first impression I get from that person. With Daniyal I was able to talk about my ambitions because he was extremely ambitious himself.

A rule I go by is if you find someone who isn't as ambitious as you are, then they aren't as strong of a line in your net as someone who is at your level of ambition. I am not saying to not be friends and create relationships with people who have less ambition as you. Network with as many people as you can. But also keep in mind that not everyone is as helpful to you because of various aspects, which includes ambition.

People want to network with somebody who has a brand. I went over a bit of branding as I narrated about *Wicked Funny*. There are many subsets within the subject of branding. There can be logos, jingles, pictures, colors, and individuals associated with a brand. People can have their own brand too. Companies are not the only ones affiliated with this idea. When you think of Mother Teresa, you formulate the idea of one of the world's greatest humanitarians, or when you think of Chris Rock, you picture one of the greatest edgy comedians of all time. Those ideas are their brands, and brands don't necessarily have to be a positive idea either. When someone talks about Hitler, or even the school bully, both of those people have a bad brand. Granted, some people have worse brands than others—Hitler, in the last example—and you do not want to have that bad brand. First impressions help with a person's brand because that's how other people remember you. Also, if you have an achievement in your specified area, then you have a brand. The way Daniyal and I marketed *Wicked Funny*'s first show was by promoting the fact we had a headliner, Drew Dunn, who had won the Boston Comedy Festival. The branding aspect of the promotion was that students at Emerson thought, "Oh, this *Wicked Funny* has professional headliners." That's what we wanted people to know about us. Drew also has a brand because he has won a comedy competition in a prominent comedy festival. We were able to use his brand as a selling point and, in turn, students had the idea *Wicked Funny* had legit headliners. These are all aspects of branding.

I've gone over charisma, ambition, and branding. I believe the most important part of networking is how refined and effective your communication skills are. You can't get anywhere if you don't know how to talk to somebody because no one will know what you're trying to do. If you met somebody who isn't able to talk to you confidently, is your first impression of them that they will help you in life? I can guarantee you that it isn't, so be friendly and communicate to people with confidence. The only way you can get better at talking is by interacting with others. Also, you can go on to YouTube and listen to professional speakers talk. There's a reason why they're called professional, and I have yet to find one who isn't amazing at communicating. When I communicate, I push myself to make a friendly environment so the conversation is nice, and I want to find agreements between the person I'm talking to and myself. The purpose of that is to create relatable topics for us to talk about. Those two tips seem like no-brainers, but I've talked to many people who don't use them and seem to be complete jerks. In the situation of finding someone who doesn't have that much to relate with, still try to make that friendly connection. But you don't have to be best of friends with that person. While you are talking to somebody, make sure you are clear with your communication, and be confident while talking, so your communication gets across perfectly. You should keep your attention on the person you're talking to so you understand what they're saying. Conversations are not always going to be like this, but try to keep it to the standard so you and the person you're talking to aren't confused about the conversation.

    Networking is complementary to success because connections can get you anywhere, and, of course, you need to connect with the right people to succeed. If you network with an owner of a company, you have more chances of getting corporate gigs than if you were to network with a cashier. I am not saying you shouldn't network with cashiers because they might have friends who are looking to hire comics. I am trying to communicate that you should find out what you want (e.g. get on corporate gigs), and network with the people who can get you there. I network with many of the security guards and cooks working at Emerson College, and they have offered me gigs at parties or events they are holding.

    Don't stop at parties. If I were to only do those parties, then I would fall into the trap of complacency. Don't let yourself be complacent because you won't progress. Play big games, and find bigger ones as you become more able. I say the word "game" because I look at life like a game. There are usually two sides: yours and whatever obstacles are in your way, and it is your intention to win this game. The bigger the tasks you take on, the higher the chances will be for you to win big games in the game of life. This relates to networking because the people you see who played big games will also help you to find big games to play, if you establish a good relationship with them. Find those people, and play those big games. It will help you out a lot, and you will find yourself more competent then you previously were.

An example of me playing a bigger game would be when I tried getting a tolerance for spice. As my ma raised me, she never fed me spicy food. She couldn't handle spice herself, so I didn't have much tolerance for it. Whenever we ate out, she would eat some of the food I ordered. I didn't like that, so I decided I needed to eat spicy food so my ma wouldn't eat it. I expanded the limits of my spice threshold by eating spicy food. I was able to eat really spicy food in a couple of months, and the best thing was that my ma couldn't eat the food I ordered because she couldn't handle it. I was able to play a bigger game, and solve a problem because of it.

There you have it. The tips I have for networking. Talk to people, and get as many connections as you can. One thing you should have when networking is your business card, or something you can give for people to remember you by. I have my own business cards, and I give them out when I'm networking. The first time I created a business card was probably at the age of 15, and it had my contact info, with a picture of the Golden Gate Bridge on it. At the back of the card was a quote from a pastor named T.D. Jakes, and it said, "I like to see myself as a bridge builder, that is me building bridges between people, between races, between cultures, between politics, trying to find common ground." I used this business card while working in politics because it was appropriate for the field I planned to enter.

My old comedic business card is a little bit more creative because of my comedic exploits. I will talk about my new one in Chapter 6 of this book. If you have ever seen it, it says my name and my contact information. There is a quote on it that I have been saying since I was 10 years old. It is, "Once you go brown, you never frown." Also, I have added pictures of three different Indian couples to represent some of my bits, which are based on my upbringing. In order, you will see a Sikh couple, a Hindu couple, and a Muslim couple, because those are the types of Indians I interacted with the most. At the back of the card is a quote from the great George Carlin, and it says, "Everyone smiles in the same language." There are pictures of people from various cultural backgrounds around that quote, and I am satisfied with the communication my business card's design gets across. It is extremely appropriate for comedy, and I suggest you create a business card that is creative and funny. Many people will remember you by it because that's what they take from a conversation they had with you.

Who are the specific people you should network in comedy with? That's a good question to be asking because you need to know who would be able to help you the most. I suggest you network with the local comics, hosts of any shows, bookers, and professional comics, when you get a chance to meet them. Start out with hosts and local comics because they are more likely to talk to you at the beginning. Once you get a better brand, club bookers and professional comics will make time to talk to you. It's not that they don't want to talk to you, but they have busy lives too. You need to give them a reason why they should invest their time in you. These connections will help you in the long run, and help you get gigs. I met a professional comic, Ezekiel Echevarria, and we talked for about 5 minutes. He helped me out with his connections in the Bay Area, and he gives me advice on my act. Make the effort to create a chance for you to talk to a club booker or professional comic, and create a great impression so they can remember you because of that. Ask a lot of questions, without sounding needy and annoying, about comedy and how to get booked. Some comics have different pieces of information to give you about getting booked, and about the comedy scene. It is good to assimilate all the information you receive from the comics you talk to, and to judge the importance of each piece of information.

I want you to write down a couple of things you can do to improve your communication skills, and how you can attract the interests of people you want to network with. Go over and write down things you can do to create a good impression in a conversation, and also figure out ways you can brand yourself as a friendly person and a great comic. I usually say, "I have a show called *Wicked Funny* at Emerson College." This sentence lets people know that I have a show, and I have also booked people on the show. I also want you to write down business card ideas, which would promote who you are. There is a list at the end of this chapter, where you can write your communication improvements, good impression tactics, branding strategies, and business card ideas. Take your time on this, and make sure your list is complete and will help you with networking.

Throughout this chapter, you have gained knowledge of the art of networking, and who to network with. The next chapter will provide information on where the best places are to network in regards to comedy, and also how you can network while learning the behind-the-scenes of comedy, which will come in handy for the future. This next chapter will help you hit two birds with one stone! Don't miss the opportunity to find out how you can get ahead with this very important step.

Comedy Is No Joke!

NETWORKING LIST

Communication Improvements:

_____
_____
_____
_____

Good Impression Tactics:

_____
_____
_____
_____

Branding Strategies:

_____
_____
_____
_____

Business Card Ideas:

_____
_____
_____
_____

Chapter 5

Two Birds with One Stone

"Work hard, be kind, and amazing things will happen to you."
– Conan O'Brien

Your inquisitive mind must be trying to guess what could possibly help you network while learning behind-the-scenes comedy. If you're thinking the answer is talking to a comedian, and asking, "What are the behind-the-scenes of comedy?" then, you are wrong. It's a good guess, but still wrong. The answer is to work or intern in a company, club, or festival dedicated to comedy. There might be some other place you can work at, but those three are the big ones. Before I started my first semester at Emerson, I applied for an internship with the Boston Comedy Festival, and I was accepted. I've had many adventures and fun experiences as an intern, and I also found my first headliner for *Wicked Funny* through the festival. I learned a lot from the festival, and I keep learning by helping them out as much as I could, because I know the festival will help me in the future.

You can work in comedy in many places, and all you have to do is just apply for the job. Comedy clubs are looking to hire security guards and people for the box office, and there are many other positions. If you are in college, the best thing you could do is apply for one of these jobs. Generally, they don't interfere with class schedules because comedy performances happen at night. You can find an internship or volunteer position at a comedy happening around your town or in your city. These are all great ways to learn the business of Comedy, and network with the professionals that perform in the club. The amount of networking you can do while working a job in comedy is eye-opening. You will find many professionals who can give you great advice on performance, getting booked, and other aspects of comedy. You can also be sure to trust this information because the professional comics have first-hand experience. It is not like basing your knowledge on the assumptions of local comics in the open mic scene.

The Boston Comedy Festival has shows throughout the year. There are ones in the actual festival, and others organized after it. My bosses, Helen and Jim, assigned me tasks to help out with the shows, and also, on the day of, they have me help set up chairs and fulfill the needs of the comics (nothing too weird though). I would tell comics, "Hey, my name is Vinny, and I work for Jim. Today, I'm going to be your right-hand man, so if you need anything, just let me know, and I'll get it done." I helped out as much as I could. This created a good impression with the comics, which played well in my favor. When I meet those comics again, then I can say, "I'm Vinny. I was your right-hand man at (insert show title). I worked under Helen and Jim." They'd probably remember me since I made that good impression.

At all the shows I've helped with, the comics performing have been extremely nice to me. They answer my questions about the comedy industry, and what steps to take that would help get my name out there. I also talked to Jim a lot because he performs stand-up professionally, and I've seen him on stage too. I couldn't stop laughing. The questions I asked Jim had to do with agents, getting gigs, submitting reels to festivals, and what to do when starting out. Jim has been very helpful with all the advice he has given me, and I have to say, it's a blessing that I was able to create such an amazing relationship with him.

I met Todd Barry once, in the Somerville Theater, and I told him, "I am your security guard for today, and I work for the comedy festival." His performance was amazing, and the really cool thing was that he came out with his Netflix special a couple of months later. It is nice knowing that I met a comic who has a Netflix special. Todd wasn't the only comic I met through the festival. I have many fun stories of my encounters with professionals. One of my favorites was when I met Tony Hinchcliffe, the guy who runs the podcast, *Kill Tony Live*. About 5 minutes before the podcast was supposed to start, I was asked to find a pair of scissors and cut up a bunch of pieces of paper. I think it was about 50 to 60 pieces, and I was able to do all that, but I don't want to do it ever again. If you aren't familiar with the podcast, Tony draws a random name from a bucket, and he has that person perform stand-up for a minute on air. Tony and his guest comics critique the stand-up set, and have a good time doing so. One of the contestants, which Tony had drawn, said in her stand-up set that the security guard (which was me) forced her to write her name down to participate in the podcast. Tony yelled, "Vinny, did you force this girl to be on my podcast?!?!?!" Of course, I didn't force her, but I think she misheard me when I was explaining how the podcast worked. Even after all that, Tony offered me an internship if I ever was to be in LA, because of how hard I worked to help out with the podcast. He's such a good guy.

Jim and I have an inside joke, where I introduce myself as a security guard. If you saw the two of us standing next to each other, you would be laughing. Jim is about 6'5", and I am about 5'8", and Jim has more weight on him. The joke started when he said, "Vinny, your job is to make sure nobody bothers the comedians, and that everyone who enters the theater has paid." I asked him, "So, am I the security guard for the show?" He answered, "Yeah, you are." I took that to mean I'd be the security guard for Jim and all the comedians at every show. I find it funny when I say, "I was a security guard for the Boston Comedy Festival."

There are many tips on how to do well in your job, and I'll go over what I did for the festival. It's interesting at the festival because I never know what's going to pop up. A comic might want something that you didn't expect they would need. Tony Hinchcliffe needed scissors, and we were in the middle of a theater. I searched all over the theater for a pair, and after I found them I cut up the paper quickly. My adrenaline was rushing throughout my search, but thankfully I found some. Before I arrive at any show, I always come prepared for these random needs. I bring a backpack with a notebook, a couple of pencils and pens, sticky notes, a sharpie, and, of course, scissors. I bring all the desk items I think will be needed for some small reason, and the list doesn't stop there. There might be a new need that arises, which you never expected. Be prepared for anything, but also don't be worried.

These situations I'm talking about aren't frequent, and if you're enjoying your time at the show, things will be great. The experience will be as fun as you make it to be. Being prepared also means to know the names and faces of the comics performing at the show. I was working at one of Jim's fundraising events, Stand-up to Cancer, and he gave me a list of comics who would be performing. I didn't fully go over the list, and I made myself look like a fool when I didn't know a comic. One more step I take is asking Jim if there are any comics not on the list that will be performing. Sometimes he tells me one or two extra comics will perform, but at Stand-up to Cancer, it was a different story. I didn't ask him, and there were three to five comics who weren't on the list. I felt extremely embarrassed when I told a comic, "I'm sorry, sir. I can't let you in unless you have a ticket." He looked at me confused, and said, "Ummm... I am one of the performers." I double-checked with a volunteer at the show, and she confirmed he was performing. It turns out the guy was Gary Gulman, a comic who has been on Last Comic Standing, and had released a Netflix special, in 2016. Always ask your boss if there are any extra performers, because you don't want to look stupid. Gary was a very nice guy, and was very understanding, so I was able to get away with that.

Always push to do the best job you can do, and when your boss assigns you a task, go above and beyond his expectations. Having that mindset will put you on his good side, and that is exactly what you want to do. An intern, or an employee who is liked by his boss, gets extra perks on the job. Once Jim asked me to set up chairs at a theater, and when I was done, I decided to clean up the messy areas of the venue. I took a broom and start sweeping, and Jim was very happy with my work ethic. Through my work, not only with the festival but with all my work experience, I have seen that there are four categories you can put a worker in. The first one is a worker who doesn't contribute anything to the team, and he's just there to get paid. That worker is not doing his job, and is putting his tasks onto others, which makes him a liability to the team. The second type is a worker who only does part of what he is told, which is better than the first but not good enough. The third is the worker who does just what he is told, which is great and very helpful to the team. The fourth one is the worker who does more than what is expected, and is more likely to have a better impression on his boss and his team. Strive to be the 4th category all the time because that's how you make the best impression on anyone. The third one is good too, but if many workers do what they're told, and just that, you have no unique aspect to your contribution. Remember that you want to be unique because that difference can give you the brand of being different and better. Be an essential part to the team. Your goal should be that the team always wants you because you do so well. With that impact, your boss will do so much for you because of how much you contribute. Find ways to improve the operating basis your team runs on. Make it more efficient or add something that can help bring about a better product. The Boston Comedy Festival has been getting many marketing and promotional ideas from me. Since I'm a college student, I market to my college peers at Emerson, and also to other colleges around Boston.

    Jim sometimes pays for my food after shows because he knows I consistently do a good job. At Stand-up to Cancer, Jim gave me a shout out at the end of the whole performance. He didn't have to do that, and the only reason he did that was because I always show up to the festival's shows and help out as much as I can. You want to get these perks because they help you imprint your picture in the minds of comics and audience members. On top of all that, you can get free food, and who doesn't like that? Jim has put me on one of his podcasts, Stand-up with a Secret, and it was a great time. These were the words he used to describe me when I was about to get on, "Our next contestant is a guy who has done so much for the comedy festival. He's always working and helping us out, and we don't know where we would be without him. Vinny Pal, everyone!"

    Be professional at work, but this doesn't mean you can't have fun.

It means, don't goof off all the time, and have the mindset you are representing whatever club or festival you work for. I know, when I'm helping Jim and Helen at a show, audience members see me as a part of the Boston Comedy Festival. So, I always set a professional tone with them, and I am always friendly. Being friendly is probably the best thing you can do when you are working with people because most people, generally, are attracted to friendly people. This can tie in with the relationship between networking and charisma.

Jim usually had me do crowd control, and I had to direct audience members to their seats. He would tell me, "Vinny, you need to have them sit from one end of a row to another. We don't have gaps in between people. We're probably going to have a full house." It was hard sometimes to get people to follow my seating directions because they might feel uncomfortable with sitting in a certain area I pointed out to them. Some audience members did not want to sit in the front because a lot of comics make fun at audience members in the front. I couldn't force them to sit there, so I decided that I shouldn't make it so strict. I let people sit in whatever rows they wanted, as long as they sat from one end of the row and filled it up gradually. The new system I created was successful, and the audience was happy with it too. I told Jim what I did, and he was happy with it too.

You might be wondering if you should do an internship or a job, because a job actually pays. Granted, some internships do pay, but they aren't as common compared to unpaid internships. If you are looking for some money, then getting a job at a club probably will help you out. My opinion is that the point of working in comedy is to learn about the organizational and business side of the art, and to network with big comedians. Let's say you are offered two positions: one from a nearby comedy festival, and another from a local club. The club is offering you $12 an hour, but the position at the festival is an unpaid internship. You do your research and find out the festival has more comics perform in it, and it is pretty prominent compared to others. I suggest you take the unpaid internship with the festival because you can make more out of the connections with the festival than the club.

Through the Boston Comedy Festival, I haven't been directly paid for my work, but I have made so many connections with comedians touring the U.S. There was this one time Jim was on a panel at Harvard, and he invited me. One of the executives of Improv Asylum was there too, and he was impressed with my professionalism. He offered me a free improv class later that month, and those classes are about $250. There are many things that can come out from your work in comedy, but you have to make sure the place you work at has a name and is known for having professionals perform there frequently. Monetary compensation shouldn't be your objective, but instead, focus on creating relationships.

I want you to write down ways you can be a worker in the fourth category, and also write down a list of materials you should bring with you before a show. There's a list on the next page you can use to write all your ideas on. After you are done with that, continue onto the next chapter, which unfolds my secrets of promotion. PROMOTION is the deciding factor of a theater with a full audience, or a theater with five people. If you want the theater full of people, then continue reading to learn how to sell out.

Comedy Is No Joke!

PREPARATION LIST

Fourth Category Ideas:

_____
_____
_____
_____
_____
_____
_____
_____

List of Materials:

_____
_____
_____
_____
_____
_____
_____
_____
_____

Chapter 6

Promotion

"Without promotion, something terrible happens... nothing!"
– P.T. Barnum

Promotion is the key action that will help you be known. The last thing you want is lack of promotion. You want to promote yourself and your show as much as possible. I promote myself through introductions. For example, when I talk to someone new, I introduce myself: "My name is Vinny," and then some where in the conversation I drop, "I'm the author of the book, *Comedy Is No Joke! A Stand-up Comic's Guide to Success.*" This promotes my book, and me, being an author of a book on comedy. Promote as much as possible because it will help you in many areas of your life, especially in comedy.

A good means of promotion is through a website. I don't suggest you get a website when you start out because you should be working on material, but as you progress, you should be thinking of creating one. There are many features to include in your website that will help with promotion. Anything that will give someone visiting your website a good impression of you would be a smart thing to add. For example, if you performed on a late night show, then having the logo of the show on your website would let people know you have good experience in comedy. Winning a festival is another example of showing your experience, and including the logo of the festival you won would be another great tactic to make you stick out. You should have a calendar on your website showing when you are performing at clubs, or performing in general, because people will know where you will be if they are interested in watching you perform.

The website should be of good quality, and it should be easy to navigate. When people look at an unattractive website or a difficult one to navigate (maybe even both), they tend to think that it's very unprofessional. The people visiting your website probably have never met you, and this is your first impression on them. Like I said before, the first impression should be a good one. Comics have funny descriptions of themselves in their biography page, but I don't think it's necessary to have a funny biography—it's up to you if you want one. The first thing a person should see on your website is either a list of credentials with a link to a video, or many testimonials of your performance. These should be a page that pops up immediately when a person first enters your website. There needs to be a button on this page that lets a visitor exit and continue exploring the rest of your website.

You don't want to be like a company who is trying to sell you something, and on their website a page pops up that doesn't have a very visible exit button. Those are the worst. The purpose of a credential page is to show you are a branded comedian.

Your website should make it so that people can contact you easily, in case they want to book you for parties or get-togethers. The exception to this is if you are a huge comedian, like Russell Peters, Dave Chappelle, or another comic of that magnitude. Those types of big comics usually have visitors contact agents, or people working for the comic. Those are my main tips for a website; the rest of the website features are up to you. Check out my website, vpalcomedy.com, to see how I incorporate my own tips.

I talked about my old business card in the fourth chapter, and its features to promote myself. I told you to write down ideas for your card, in that chapter, and while you are reading this paragraph, and the next, refer to that list a few times. The business card is another way of creating a lasting impact, and if you do it right, many people will remember you. The most basic thing a business card should have is your information. You can put whatever information you think is necessary on your card. On my new one, I include my website title, my social media handles, and my book's title. I don't include my phone number anymore because I don't know in whose hands my number will end up. I do have my email on there so people can reach me through that. I do include pictures on my business card, and I chose them to match what type of comedy I perform. I have pictures of people from many cultural backgrounds because I do a lot of cultural comedy. I also have a picture of three Indian families, from different religious backgrounds, to depict the families I was raised around, and also the families who have influenced my comedic style. My card contains, on all versions of it, my own quote, "Once you go brown, you never frown." I have a secondary quote from someone famous, and on my old one, I chose to use a quote from George Carlin.

I believe the more creative your business card is, the higher the chance you will have of people remembering you. Take your time planning the design of your business card because it's not a huge rush, and you want it to be good. The design of my old comedic business card took me a while, and I wasn't able to think of anything until I had a talk with my girlfriend. I asked her, "Em, I need help thinking of a business card idea." We play a game where she gives me three words, and I try to write a comedy that relates to all those words. I asked her this time, "Can you give me only one word?" She came up with the word "world" and about five ideas popped into my mind when I read it. I picked the one that I described to you in Chapter 4, and I kept its foundation for my new business card. A business card should be able to promote who you are and what you do, at first glance. The professional title I have on my card is Comedic Entrepreneur & Author, which makes it obvious to others what I have a relation with, and that I'm an author. You can write down stand-up comic. I wanted to be more creative, so I use that title.

I remember showing my business card to my mom, and she said, "You should have put down Comedic Doctor. It would have been much better." She has always wanted me to go into medicine, and I told her that most patients probably wouldn't want a doctor who jokes with them during their physical. Just imagine a doctor saying, "I'm sorry, but you have a bad hernia, and when I say bad, I mean it's probably the worst one I've ever seen. You might need an expensive surgery." You would be frightened half to death, and you would be very angry if the doctor ended with, "I am just kidding. It's only a sore." Everything would exacerbate if he also included, "Your health insurance provider doesn't include jokes with the physical exams. You're going to have to pay an extra $500 for that one." It's an easy way of making money in comedy, but an easier way to lose your license.

Social media is a very important way of getting yourself out there. Most people use social media, and the ones who don't are usually old grandmas and grandpas who don't care about your comedy. As I scroll through my Facebook feed, I usually see many comics posting their upcoming events, pictures of the venue they just performed in, pictures of them with other comics they performed with, and, of course, jokes. I also see comics use their social media accounts like normal people. That list of what a comic posts shows things comics post in addition to that.

All these media outlets are your allies, and if you use them right, they will help you gain an avid group of followers. Your purpose for using social media, as a comic, would be to promote yourself. I think that's the purpose of a lot of people who use social media. They use it to promote their lives and tell the world a lot of unnecessary stuff, like a friend posting that he hates the rain. Well, random social media user, you should move to the desert. Promote yourself as a great comic, and have posts to show how awesome you are. Not all your posts have to be a comedy. That isn't the message I want to send; there is more to your life than comedy, so there are more things to post about. I bet someone who follows you would love to see your cat do a neat trick.

The first time I met Jim at the Boston Comedy Festival, he asked me if I was interested in stand-up. I told him yes, and he told me I should master social media. He also emphasized to never buy followers, and that the expense is a waste of money. I'm relaying the information to you, so don't waste your money on fake followers. You told me that the fake followers you buy don't like your posts, and they don't share them either. Remember, the purpose of your social media is to promote yourself—how can you promote yourself if you don't get likes and shares? There are better ways for you to spend your money than on expenditures for fake followers. Comedy isn't a very lucrative industry at first, so you should be investing money in other resources. If you do think purchasing fake followers is a great way to utilize your money, then go for it. But don't come crying to me when Ch3wbaKca13!, JDrew57, and all the other Instagram users you bought aren't liking your posts.

Comics who have a show have another responsibility on their hands. They don't only have to promote themselves but their show as well. Promoting your show can be done on your own social media, and you should also have a page just for your show. Daniyal and I promote *Wicked Funny* on our Facebook pages, and on any Facebook groups we are a part of. *Wicked Funny* has its own Facebook page because it can get followers who will have notifications about upcoming shows, without having to be friends with Daniyal and me. The separate page can get the show promoted to more people and, in turn, we will have more people at the show. I have a friend who runs a mic, and he gets many people to that mic because he has a page of 730 followers. It's not his personal page. It's just for the mic, and it's a huge turnout. It should be your goal to get a lot of followers on your show's Facebook page so that page does more of the promotion for the show than your personal one. Your personal page should mainly be about you and what you've been doing in comedy. Your show is a part of your comedic resume, and it's okay to promote it, but your upcoming performances at clubs are more important on your personal page to show people how much you are doing in comedy.

One of the minor ways of promoting is by getting your name in newspaper or magazine articles. The reason why I say this is minor, compared to the others, is because someone who is starting out should be more focused on social media, a website, and their business card. Getting in a newspaper or magazine article is pretty amazing, but that's not where the focus should be at the beginning. If you are pretty big, then surely, getting in a magazine is a step up. When you do get in an article, you should have your social media handles somewhere in the article because you can then get more followers, which means more promotion. It's cool to be able to say that you have been mentioned in an article in a paper like the *Boston Globe*, but you should also get in an article from any source, because it means more publicity. Any means of getting your name out there in society is an opportunity you should take.

Testimonials are great for you to collect and show on your website or on your social media. What is the definition of a testimonial? It's a statement describing your qualifications or character. They are extremely important to have. When you are looking for new restaurants to check out, don't you look at reviews of the restaurant? Those are testimonials, and now you can see how important they are. Someone visiting your website would be impressed if you had many testimonials, and with how great your performances are. I think stand-up comics should have a couple of funny testimonials, even if they don't have anything to do with their act.

I was on a podcast once, and the basic premise of the podcast was for a couple of professional comedians to guess a secret you have. Patty Ross, who has been on many stand-up networks, and in a couple of movies, was on the panel of comics. They were trying to guess my secret, which was that I was involved in a hit and run with a cow in India. When Patty heard I did that, she said, with the most pronounced Boston accent, "He killed a cow with a car in India!" I use that testimonial comically to show how crazy I am. I mix that one in with a couple of other testimonials that talk about my performance, so people know that the Patty Ross testimonial is a joke. I wasn't the driver in that hit and run, but since I was a part of it, I could have gotten into a whole lot of trouble. I don't want people in India to think I am a horrid cow killer. I blame it all on the cow for not moving out of the way.

For this chapter, I want you to write down ideas to help your promotion. It could be on a website, and what I suggested to add in one. As you continue reading, you will find out my tips on keeping a

Promotion

loyal fan base, and how to get people attracted to, and stay interested in, you and your comedy. Without fans, you are nothing, so continue to the next chapter to find out what you can do to perpetuate your fan base.

PROMOTION IDEAS

Chapter 7

Loyal Fan Base

"The fans in Canada have been there since day one. They're the originals. When people say that's your roots, that's literally my roots. I've just cut this tree off and replanted it somewhere else, and it started growing. But the roots are there."
— Russell Peters

Russell was able to keep a loyal fan base in Canada, even though he branched out as an international phenomenon. That's mighty impressive. Fans are what constitutes a comedian's main line of income, and determines the amount of fun he has at a show. A comic will enjoy performing because there are many people there to watch him. Not having fans is the worst. Imagine a football game with no one at the stadium. I couldn't imagine having fun at a 49er game without anyone there to watch it with me. I mean, if you are a loner, then that would be the perfect way for you to watch a live game, but for normal people, it isn't. It is the same concept with comedy because you don't want to be at a show that has low attendance. Shows with low attendance are like open mics with five other comics, especially for a show you don't want. The more fans there are, the more fun the show will be. Thinking back at many award-winning speeches by actors, comedians, or any job related to show business, I always hear the fans getting thanked.

Without the fans, the performer is nothing—there's no one interested and watching that performer. A great way to keep a loyal fan base is to preserve a good image of yourself. I have to admit that statement is completely subjective because a good image is pictured differently amongst various groups. The image of Robert Downey Jr. can be seen as a good one to many people, including myself, but can be seen as bad for others. It really depends on a person's taste, and everyone has a different taste. Don't try to create an image that appeals to everyone; it is hard to do without sacrificing some of your integrity. You should try to have a first impression that does appeal to all people, but you develop an image as people get to know you more. It's up to you how you want to portray yourself because that's a precursor of who will be your fan. If you are the energetic type, you will tend to have more fans with high energy. If you do a lot of edgy humor, you will get all sorts of people following you, and many of them probably are impressed with your wit shown in your edgy humor. What you put out in the universe, you will get back. It's the law of attraction.

Many celebrities and performers can lose a majority of their fan base in an instant. If they do something bad, like saying something hurtful, then they can end their career. Remember the Michael Richards incident? If you don't know him, he played Kramer in Seinfeld. He ruined his career because he uttered racial slurs at an audience member who was heckling. You don't hear about him as much, unless a comic is making fun of that incident. Before that, he was a huge star, and many people would want to watch him. Now, not many people want to, because when they hear Michael Richards, or Kramer, they associate him with this racist incident. You can discern what is bad and what is good, so don't do anything dumb.

The image you portray ties in with branding; your image, and what you do, defines who you are. A great example of a comic with a great and lasting image is Jon Stewart. He's not as big in comedy as he used to be because he contributes much of his time to politics. But his brand as a comic and a good person keeps growing because of it. His fans love the fact he's doing so much in politics. They are exhilarated when he makes appearances on any show. You're never going to hear a long-time fan of the *Daily Show* say, "I forgot about Jon Stewart." He has managed to keep himself in the hearts of many fans, even though he doesn't do as much in comedy. That's the image you want.

You also want an image where people know you very well, and they want to watch your comedy. A great example of a comic who had this is Moms Mabley. She was one of the most influential black comics of the 20th century. She had so many black people attend her shows because when they heard Moms Mabley was performing at a local venue, then they would rush to buy tickets. She was that influential in the black community during her lifetime, and her image was adored by so many. Whoopi Goldberg directed a documentary called *Moms Mabley: I Got Somethin' to Tell You*. You will hear black comics, performers, singers, etc. talk about how they snuck into the living room to hear Moms Mabley's records as kids because she was so funny. They had to sneak around because her comedy was a little crass, and their parents didn't want them listening to crass humor. It should be your goal to have such an image where people want to risk listening to your comedy, even if they get grounded or beat for doing it. That's true loyalty.

When you're booked at parties or at clubs, be as nice as you can because your kindness will create a good effect on others. People will remember you for that, and they will recommend you to others. When they talk about you, it will be words of praise, not critique. If you're at a party, don't be someone with the idea, "I'm the star of this party, and people have to treat me the best." You're just being pretentious, and that's the opposite of what you should be. Have nice communication with everybody, and have a fun time. The loyalty of your fans will grow when they experience your kindness. It's different for big timers, like Kevin Hart, because their name attracts fans. When you're starting to perform at pre-booked shows and clubs, what I've told you is useful.

Keeping your fans in the loop will keep you relevant in their lives. There are many ways of doing this, and the most efficient is through email updates. Gather as many email addresses as you can, so you can email your fans when you have a show. This will keep you in their minds, and if they're close by, then they might come by and watch your show. Don't email people too much because it might get a little annoying. You might think this might be hard for a comic who has many shows in the month, and if you're a comic who fits that description, then email a list of shows you will be performing that month. There are other ways to send out the least amount of emails with the most amount of promotion. That's a strategy I know works for many comics. You can also use your social media to promote your shows, and those posts will help you diminish the need to email a lot. This doesn't mean you shouldn't email. It means you should use social media to enhance your promotion alongside your emails. This tip will help you stay relevant with your fan base, and that factors into their loyalty.

Do more than what is expected, always. Think of how you can create a great experience for your fans. Many people have done things like giveaways, discounts, and other fun prizes. I think it would be best for you to reward fans who have been following you for a while. You'll make them feel special, and they will keep staying beside you as a fan. If you have a person who keeps booking you after parties, it would be a good notion for you to do something nice for them. They probably won't be expecting it, and you'll create an amazing impact. You can give them the show for half off, or give them free tickets to the next show in their area.

The last point I want to make is, when you feel unhappy, do whatever it takes to still do a good job. You might have a bad day, and that will affect your mood, but people aren't paying to see a moody comic. The only scenario I could think of, where that would be okay, is if you played a moody character in your stand up bits. Your job, as a professional, is to make sure your audience doesn't think you did a horrible job. It's hard for some people to do their job—in this case, it is comedy—when they aren't happy. There are a couple ways to help with this, and one of them is to fill your thoughts with the happy things in your life. Another is to go over your purpose for doing comedy: you're here to make people laugh. Think about how great it will feel to know you did a good job, especially on top of having a bad day. That type of work deserves to be commended because not everyone can do it. Strive to be that comic who can perform a set hilariously, even when he's down. This will give your fans the impression you can do a good job all the time, and that's something a comic should be proud of.

I want you to think of ideas you can use to help create a loyal fan base. I focused on the subject of creating an image, at the beginning of this chapter. Figure out ways you can create an image that you like and that fits with your integrity. Think of special gifts for fans who keep booking you, or even kind words you can say to people to give them a nice impression. Also, strategize your emails so they're efficient and keep you relevant. There's a list of them in this chapter, which you can write your ideas on.

The next chapter will talk about something very important to stand-up. You will find my tips on writing and gathering material, and what I do to create my bits. This chapter is something you want to read now; because, without material, you can't perform stand-up. To find out how your life, and everything around you, is full of material, keep moving on to the next chapter, and you will be writing a bunch of bits in no time.

IDEAS TO KEEP A LOYAL FAN BASE

Image:
_____
_____
_____
_____
_____

Special Gifts:
_____
_____
_____
_____
_____

Email Efficiency:
_____
_____
_____
_____
_____

Chapter 8

Material and Writing

"If you think something is funny, it's funny. If the audience doesn't laugh, that doesn't mean it's not funny; that just means that audience has no idea what you are talking about."
– Chris Rock

    Writing and material go hand in hand. In stand-up, we define material as the subject matter you use in bits. You need material in order to perform stand-up because, without it, you have nothing to tell your audience. There are all sorts of types of material, and as you perform more, you realize what material you are to perform. Personally, I perform cultural material, life stories, self-deprecation, and odd things I observe. The two I perform the most are cultural and my life stories. Writing is used to create jokes out of the material a comic thinks of. You need both to have a prepared stand-up set.
    How do you gather material? There is material everywhere around you. You can use anything in plain sight for a stand-up bit. Jot down anything you see or think might have comedic potential. ALWAYS have a notebook on you, or your phone on you, to write down notes. I still have notes from three years ago, and I use them for bits I write now. You might not be able to make a great joke out of something at first, but you will in the future. It took me a while to write down a funny joke about the hit and run I had with a cow in India. That concept is extremely funny, but I couldn't say, on stage, "You know what's funny? I killed a cow in India!" The writing of the joke should focus on

formatting the words in such a way that the audience isn't expecting the punchline. When I say there is material everywhere, I literally mean everywhere. I was in my dorm room, and I looked at my roommate's microwave and saw that one of the buttons was labeled "baked potato". I thought to myself, "Aren't baked potatoes baked, not microwaved? Hence the title, baked potatoes." There are many other instances where things like that have happened to me. This is where most observational comedy comes from, and your observations of the people and environment around you is a great tool for finding new material.

Your life and beliefs are full of material for you to exploit. A person who says that they don't have much to use from their life isn't thinking hard enough. Everyone has an abundance of material from their past experiences. Middle school was probably full of things you can use. I use a lot of material about my ma and how she raised me, and about the Indian culture and other Asian cultures, as well as crazy stories about my friends, my adventures in boarding school, my experiences with Hinduism, and many other things. What I've noticed is audiences respond better to bits pertaining to my life. I had a guy tell me after a show that he was extremely impressed with the Hindu and Muslim jokes I had in my set, and it was because I used my experiences as a Hindu, and my interactions with Muslims.

I did change things to make stories funny in a stand-up setting, but the foundation of those bits was based on personal experiences. Use personal experiences as much as you can because that's material waiting to be crafted in your writing. I met Ice-T, and I showed him my business card. He read my quote, "Once you go brown, you never frown," and he called me a mothafucka. It's normal for a person to be offended when they get called a mothafucka or mafucker, but I felt honored when Ice-T called me that. I tell people with pride, "You know the guy Ice-T? He called me a mothafucka once." One of my goals is to get called mothafucka by Ice Cube, Snoop Dogg, Dr. Dre, 50 cent, and DMX. There is so much comedic potential in all of that. You can think about family members and how they act, or something you used to do as a kid that you now can't believe you did. There is comedy in all of that. You just need to think hard to find it.

I have heard many people say that comics shouldn't perform certain jokes because they are too offensive, but I disagree with that. I tell people that I do the material I want to do, and no one can tell me not to perform a joke. Unless someone booked me at a party, and they had certain boundaries I couldn't pass, then I might make an exception. For example, I wouldn't perform off-color jokes at a kid's birthday party. As a comic, you should be taking advantage of the First Amendment, and write material that you want, and perform as much as you want.

Test the audience before performing an edgy joke because you don't want the audience to be in a bad mood. That would ruin the whole performance. A great advantage of not performing first at a comedy show is that you can observe how the crowd reacts to the jokes of the comic performing. Do what you think is funny to you—it is your comedy. There is a point where you are performing for your audience, but if an audience has paid to hear your jokes at a club, then they should be prepared to hear some crass material. Stick to your integrity, and don't let anyone convince you to change your act into something that isn't you. Comedy is very subjective, and different funny bones react to certain jokes differently.

There were a couple of times when I got into trouble for the material I did at my high school because it was too crass. I should have known that I would get in trouble. It was a school event, and the comedy I perform in a bar is going to be taken at a different angle at a school. This was all my bad, but it didn't stop me from continuing to perform the material elsewhere. There was a staff member who said I should change my comedic style because it was too crass. I didn't do that because she compared me to Jerry Seinfeld. I don't want to perform the stuff Jerry does—I'm not Jerry. He's a great comic, but we have different styles. I respectfully told that staff member I couldn't change it. Those same jokes I got in trouble for are the ones people have laughed at in many shows. Perform what you know is true, and perform comedy that is fun for you. Don't be somebody you're not.

My high school was so great because there were opportunities to do various projects, and from the various projects, I have gathered material. I have worked under a couple of politicians, ran an exhibition for NASA moon rocks, participated in a comedy workshop, and many other things. You might be thinking, "Wow! He got to see NASA moon rocks?" It was super cool, but NASA needs to start giving out bigger portions. I swear, I could have mistaken those rocks as Fruity Pebbles. I am not trying to dis the rocks because it was awesome holding a case of moon rocks worth over 5 million dollars. It was strange to me that a couple of small rocks were worth 5 million dollars. Since that's the price for those rocks, I think if NASA sold all their moon rocks, they would make enough money to help the U.S. get out of debt.

Comics, throughout the ages, have come up with a plethora of techniques to create new material. Many techniques for gathering material can be found on the internet, but I will tell you a couple I use. I write down 20 words on one side of a page, and 20 words on the other. I draw lines connecting those words, and I think of a creative concept that relates to them. You will find some funny and outlandish topics through this technique, which helps you to be unique and surprising.

Another one I frequently use is I take a subject and draw a circle over it. On the borders of the circle, I draw lines extending outwards. Each of those lines has another word I associate with the main subject. I try to come up with stories or facts between the main subject and the associated words. When I think of cool stories or facts, I begin writing different ways to format them into a stand-up bit.

My mom and teachers told me to read a lot of books, but I never listened to them. I regret that because some material I write comes from reading books on subjects such as history, biology, physics, food, cinematography, etc. Being more knowledgeable about the world gives you more material to work with, so read as much as you can. Books on animals intrigue me the most. I read once about a species of bird that vomits on predators as a sign of self-defense. I think finding a way to learn this bird's survival mechanism would be way cheaper than paying for classes to become a black belt in karate.

Your significant other is another great source for finding material.

Material and Writing

I play a game with my girlfriend, where I ask her for three words to make a joke. She picks words that have no relation whatsoever, and I believe she does that on purpose. It's sometimes annoying, but some of my good jokes were created from the words she gave me. Many comics take opportunities to make fun of their relationship, which does get a good laugh now and then. I remember the first pre-booked show I performed in. There was a comedian making fun of how her 33-year-old boyfriend was still into video games, and couldn't do the dishes. I didn't want to break it to her that video games are for all ages. I remember beating old Indian Uncles at baseball on Wii Sports, and they would say, "If this was cricket, you would lose in a heartbeat."

I use stories of my relationship in my comedy a lot, but I don't sarcastically demean her. I don't like performing jokes of that nature. She likes to correct my English when I use bad grammar, or when I use a word incorrectly. If you ever talked to me, you would never guess English was my second language. I learned Bengali first, but I started to forget it as I learned English. But the way I speak English is heavily influenced by how my family speaks it. Bengalis use some English words differently than how they are defined. I am still figuring out that some words I have used my entire life, in a certain way, are incorrect. It's so weird. Imagine if you found out that a word, which you thought you knew perfectly, was actually different from the actual definition.

It's so mind-boggling. My mom taught me that the word toupee meant a beanie, and it was pronounced *two-pee*. A couple of months ago, my girlfriend and I were talking about my baby pictures, and I said, "I used to wear toupees a lot." She looked at me confused, and then told me the actual definition of toupee, and how to say it. My girlfriend changed my life forever in just a split second. She revealed I used the word toupee incorrectly for about 15 years! I still say it the way my mom does because the actual pronunciation is way too weird for me. My girlfriend helps me a lot when it comes to gathering material, and that's one reason why I love her. I suggest you find someone who loves you for your comedy, and is excited to help with material.

Write as much as you can. You don't need to write a joke every day. You can write a concept, or something you saw that you think could be funny, and take some time later to write out a joke on that concept. When I first started, I asked comics for tips, and many of them said to write as much as possible. I try to write as much as I can, every day. It's fine if you can't think of how to make that concept into a bit. Keep it, and look back at it in the future. I still look back at notes I have kept for years.

There are many specific strategies to use in joke writing. The basic format of a stand-up joke is set up and, then, the punchline. The information I'm going to tell you is what I learned from Craig Fox, back when I met him. In the setup, you have the topic and your premise. The topic is what is being talked about in the joke, and the premise is your hypothesis or opinion of the subject. The punchline is the funny part, and there are a couple of techniques for this. I will go over the ones I use the most. There's a classic punchline, which makes the setup funny and logical. A great example of this would be when Chris Rock said, "People say young black men are an endangered species. That's not true because endangered species are protected by the government."

Some comedians use impersonations to make their bit funny. Russell Peters does this a lot with his various ethnic characters, especially when he portrays his father. A "tag" is another punchline, right after the original one, which doesn't need a new setup. When you write a full set, write the jokes in a flow that is smooth. That is my personal preference, but some comics have different strategies with their flow, and it works with their craft. Find out how you can incorporate your old material with your new material, or see if you can add a tag to an old joke. They're all aspects to create a smooth flow.

Create a list full of your personal beliefs and your life experiences, to use as material for future bits. I want you to also find things in your environment that you find interesting and have some comedic potential. Write down at least five beliefs or experiences, and five interesting things in your environment. Once you've finished that, then take some time to write a joke out of a couple of those ideas. It would

Material and Writing

be awesome if you could write three jokes from your list. I have provided space in which to write, at the end of this chapter.

The next chapter will be on another key essential to stand-up. You will be reading about my tips and experiences on performance and polishing. If you want to get your sets to another level of funny, you are going to need to read the next chapter. Once you have written your jokes for this chapter, get started on the next one. There's no fun having a bunch of written material without knowing what to do with it!

Comedy Is No Joke!

NEW MATERIAL

Joke 1:

_____
_____
_____
_____
_____

Joke 2:

_____
_____
_____
_____
_____

Joke 3:

_____
_____
_____
_____
_____

Chapter 9

Performing and Polishing

*"All I need to make a comedy is a park,
a policeman, and a pretty girl."*
– Charlie Chaplin

Chaplin was so polished with his comedic ideas that he only needed those three things to make a comedy! The only way to polish your material is by performing it on stage, and where you perform is up to your preferences. I know a lot of comics who are full of energy on stage, and I know many who are deadpan. I have met a couple who act as a certain character on stage, and they are that character for their whole bit. There are many aspects to performing, but before you explore them, you need to get on stage. Some places where you go, you won't perform on a real stage, but perform as much as you can anywhere.

Stage time is what every comic should want. The moment you have an opportunity to perform, seize it. Get as much stage time as you can throughout the week. As you start out, attend as many open mics as you can. More open mics mean more time for you to craft your material and experiment with it. In the first chapter, you wrote down a list of all mics around you, and you should have found ways to fit attending those mics in your schedule. Performing at open mics is a great way to accumulate stage time, but there are many other ways too. Pre-booked shows are another great way to get stage time, and as you get better, you will get booked on more shows. The information on mics and pre-booked shows should be familiar to you because you read about them in the first and second chapter.

When I met Eugene Mirman, who is the voice actor of Gene, in Bob's Burgers, he told me to perform as much as I can because that's what he did in order to be where he is now. It's easier to get extra stage time when you are in college because most colleges have clubs that organize stand-up shows. Colleges with comedy programs, like Emerson, Columbia College of Chicago, and Humber College in Toronto, are likely to have many stand-up shows for their students to perform in. Take advantage of those opportunities when you are in college! The extra stage time will take you a long way.

Create your own stage time. The first thing that probably comes to mind, when you read that, is creating your own mic or show. That's true because having your own show grants you the power to have as much stage time to your heart's content. You don't want to do too much because people won't drop the mic if they don't get an ample amount of time. Since I co-produce *Wicked Funny Show*, I get to decide how much time I have on stage. That extra stage time helps me a lot with my craft, and I get a lot of extra stage time because of the show. Starting your own show is one way of creating more stage time, but there's also another way I use. I network a lot, and I tell people I'm available to perform at parties and get-togethers.

The best part about getting booked at parties is that I am usually the only comic there, so I get a lot of time to perform. You can get 30 minutes at a party; maybe even more. That's a lot of time to perform material that has worked, and to try out material that is new. There are many other ways of creating more stage time. The most common ways I observed and used are creating your own show and trying to get booked at parties. Once you get well-established, more people will come to you or visit your website to get booked. When you become extremely good, some people will probably have to go through your agent, but that's deep into your comedy career.

Is it a good idea to perform new material at a party or at a booked show? I told you, in Chapter 2, that I recommend you do polished material at pre-booked shows because you perform at them as much as at open mics, at least for the beginning of your career. If you're yearning to try some new material, then go for it. That decision is all up to you. I don't always perform only polished material at pre-booked shows. When I don't, I strategically plan which jokes I perform, at which moments because I don't want to do five straight unpolished, new jokes in a row since I don't know what the reaction will be. Everyone does this differently. I open up with a joke I have done for a while and, after that lands, I perform a new joke. Once I break the ice with the audience, I perform two new jokes, and then two polished jokes, and I keep going in that order. This technique isn't a law you need to follow. It's something I use that has helped me in the past, and I am giving it to you so you have an idea of a structure to use when you are trying to integrate new jokes into a set. I suggest you preserve the flow of your bit, so insert new jokes in areas where the flow won't be interrupted.

    Performing and getting stage time are two things that can help you most with polishing. There are many factors that play into polishing your bit. The first one is being concise. Bits containing many words tend to lose the audience's attention. Have you ever been in a class lecture where the teacher goes on and on and on about stuff you're never going to use in your life? You were probably sitting there bored, and impatiently waiting to get out of class. Think of a wordy bit like that. You are saying so many words, and your audience is waiting for that punchline. If you keep them waiting for too long, they don't even care for the punchline. Even when you say it, they probably won't last because they're too bored. A bit shouldn't be so quick that it flies over the heads of your audience, but it shouldn't be too long either.

    As you perform, you realize what words are extraneous, and find clever ways to replace them. There will be many instances where you'll find yourself deleting many sentences in a bit you wrote, after you have performed it. I edit my old bits because I find new and funnier ways to perform them. Recently, I took a bit that was originally a minute and a half, and I cut it down to 45 seconds by getting rid of some unnecessary sentences, which helped keep the audience's attention up as I performed it. That joke has done way better now than it used to. Be as concise as you can be, and you will find your audience more attentive, and you will create more time to perform other jokes in your sets.

Timing is very important when it comes to polishing your bits. I've heard some comics say it's the most important part of comedy. Another good reason to perform your polished jokes at open mics is to keep finding ways to improve your timing. I believe that you can improve something even if it is good quality, especially timing. My biggest problem when it came to timing was that I would say my jokes way too fast. I remember one of my friends telling me he couldn't understand what I was saying because I spoke so fast. Also, I was doing a workshop with Eddie Brill; he was a booker, and he also warmed up the crowd for *The David Letterman Show,* for 17 years. He told me that my bit was funny, but I didn't give enough time for the joke to land on the audience. I wasn't speaking fast because I was nervous on stage, but because I usually speak fast in a normal conversation. It took a bit of time, but I now perform at a moderate pace. When I started tackling this problem, I would keep in mind to not talk so fast, and I would deliberately and obviously slow down my speaking pace. The new pace I started to perform with became more natural over time. Personally, I put timing above being concise because, in my opinion, it ranks above how many words you use. Working on being economical with my words in my bits wouldn't solve my problem of talking too fast.

A big problem I had on stage was getting the mic off the microphone stand with ease. You would think that it is super easy, but I would always find a way to get the mic's wire tangled. It wasn't a good start to my set when I would be trying to figure out how to get the mic out of the stand. It was unprofessional, and it made the audience think I wasn't confident on stage. That's the last thing you want because if the audience senses that you are uncomfortable, then they will probably not laugh at your set. There was this one time at an open mic where I tried taking off the mic, but I used so much force that I took the stand off its base. The stand was probably loose because it's really hard to get one out of its base. That probably won't happen to you because it's a very rare situation. It was a nice time because the comics at the mic were laughing at the whole scenario, and I decided to hold the mic stand while I was performing. In most performances, comics put the mic stand to the side, but that is only if the stand has a base it can rest on. It was a fun time, but now I know how to properly handle a mic and its stand. The only way to get comfortable with the mic stand is to practice taking a mic off of it. The easiest way to do this is by attending open mics, and taking the mic off the stand. You can also find a friend or family member who has a mic, and a microphone stand, who would let you practice using theirs. As you develop your sets, you'll find ways of using the mic stand as a prop, or using the microphone to change the intonation and volume of your voice.

    A great stage presence is essential to comedic success. Having a great stage presence is an awesome skill because it can be used in so many different fields of life. I went over my stage presence stories in a previous chapter, so I won't rewrite and remind myself of the times I performed with terrible stage presence. There have been times when I have said a punchline, and no one has laughed. I used to say, "Oh, crap, that didn't work." Don't say anything like that because it makes you seem smaller. What I do is just go on to the next bit, and learn from what just happened so I can rework the bit for later.

    Another thing to remember is that not every joke works for every crowd. You might perform an extremely funny joke, but the audience doesn't have the same sense of humor as you. That's why it's good to read the audience or observe what they respond to from other comics before you perform your jokes. As you keep performing, you will be more comfortable on stage. What I did was just focus on stage presence as I was trying to improve it. I would get on stage and focus on being there comfortably while performing my jokes. I didn't care if my jokes landed or not. I just wanted to establish a great stage presence. It helped me a lot, and my stage presence is way better than it used to be. I still try to improve it today because, like I said before, there's always room for improvement.

Comedy Is No Joke!

Playing a character in your stand-up adds a lot to your set. Impersonations add an extra level of funny to your set. Jim Carrey, Robin Williams, Russell Peters, and the rising star, Jimmy O. Yang, all do this in their stand-up. Jim Carrey goes all out when it comes to playing a character. His facial and physical expressions always find a way to make me laugh as he plays a certain character. He blows everything out of proportion, which is one of the reasons why he's a comedic genius. While he was still alive, Robin Williams was able to play so many different characters in his stand-up. One of my favorite bits of all time is him joking about the creation of golf. If you haven't seen it, check it out on YouTube when you get the chance. He plays a couple of characters in there so well, and his delivery and story behind the creation of golf are hilarious. Russell Peters is great with accents, and he portrays many ethnic groups accurately in his comedy. Because it's so accurate, he is extremely funny. He emphasizes each culture's habits as he plays a character, and that emphasis attracts the laughter. I love how Jimmy O. Yang portrays his father because I have met many dads just like that, and it's hilarious how accurate Jimmy is.

I do play characters myself, and the most common character in my sets is my ma. I've mentioned her a lot, so that shouldn't be a big surprise. It's hard not to make comedy bits out of my relationship with my ma. She's a typical Bengali mom, and if you don't know what that means, let me provide the real definition of a Bengali mom. In my ma's case, it means an Indian from West Bengal, who is so down to earth that it hurts. She is also loving in a way that is painful but it helps her kid in the future, and she speaks in the range of a soprano 24/7, sings in the shower loud enough for it to be her kid's alarm clock, is extremely superstitious that she makes a gypsy look normal, and she persistently works hard to make her kid happy. That's your lesson on *Bengali moms 101*. On top of all this, my ma happens to be 4 foot 7 (she's legally a midget!), and she's named after the smallest finger, except it is spelled Pinki instead of pinky. I think the Hindu gods wanted me to be a comedian, so they decided to put me with the perfect ma, who's full of comedic material. Go to notjokebook.com to get a free recording of how I create a character for my stand-up!

Performing and Polishing

The comics I named before aren't always in character their whole set. They just play characters. There are some comics who are a different character the moment they step on stage. Bobcat Goldthwait used to do that all the time. He was on the Police Academy series, and he would play a crazy guy all the time. When I say all the time, I mean he would play it in a stand-up and on late night interviews. For the longest time, I actually thought he wasn't acting as that character but was just being himself. That all changed when I met him at the *Stand Up for Cancer* show, and he was one of the nicest and calmest guys I have ever met. He stopped playing the crazy character a while ago, but I didn't know that. There are many stand-ups who play characters, and if you want to master characters in your sets, perform as much as you can.

During a performance, I always open with a joke that I know has landed many times before, and I close with a joke that has also landed many times. You want to break the ice between you and the audience once you start performing. The best way to do that is to open with a funny joke, so the audience knows you are actually funny. The way I plan out my set is by putting my new and less polished jokes in the middle, so if they don't land, then I have funny stuff at the end to get the audience laughing. But not all comics perform in that way because everyone has their own style. Jim McCue is a type of comedian called a crowd worker because he asks the crowd questions, and creates jokes based on an audience member's answers. Most of the work I've seen Jim do is improvised on the spot, and he is very good at it. It takes a lot of practice and knowledge to get that good, so if you do want to be a crowd worker, or have those skills under your belt, you need to perform a lot. The gist of this whole chapter is if you want to be better at stand-up, and have polished jokes, you need to get as much stage time as you can.

Take some time, and delete or replace extraneous words in the three jokes from the last chapter. Once you finish that, create a list of attributes you want to improve in your sets. It could be about what I went over in this chapter, which was timing, getting the mic off its stand, stage presence, playing a character, being concise, and opening/closing your sets with funny jokes. Keep this list handy when you start performing, so you remember what you want to work on. There's a list at the end of this chapter for you to use.

The next and final chapter is about getting good vs getting big. There's a difference between both of those terms, and you will need to know that before you embark on your journey. You will learn what your priority needs to be within this concept, and what will come about, eventually, as you follow my guidelines in the next chapter. You don't want to wait because this concept is one of the most important ones in stand-up.

Performing and Polishing

NEW MATERIAL

Joke 1:
_____
_____
_____
_____

Joke 2:
_____
_____
_____
_____

Joke 3:
_____
_____
_____
_____

Attributes You Want to Improve:
_____
_____
_____
_____

Chapter 10

Getting Good vs Getting Big

"Be so good they can't ignore you."
– Steve Martin

You don't want to spend 40 hours a week at a job you hate, and you're only staying with that job because you have a stable line of income. You're not going to be happy in life. Doing what you love professionally opens up a door to a world of happiness. You just need to be good at what you love because, if not, customers won't spend their money on your product. In the list of things I love to do, stand-up is ranked somewhere at the very top. I perform stand-up as much as I can, and I have many jokes that are polished. Every day, I push myself to do better because I want to have many good jokes under my belt. What does good mean? In regards to stand-up, it means you're funny. There's nothing more to it than that. You want to make every audience think, "Wow! I had such a great time. The comic was so funny!" That should be your goal for every show or mic you do. If you don't wow the crowd one night, don't beat yourself up over it. There's no use in complaining about spilled milk.

Learn how you can improve your performance, and keep hustling. Your priority in comedy should be to find out how to be funny, or funnier, on stage. You want to be good. When you are good, people will be racing see your shows and book you for parties. I was talking to one of the founders of the Cambridge Jazz Festival about his endeavors in jazz. During the conversation, he told me, "You want to practice your craft till you get good because, when you get an opportunity to show off your skill, you want to have enough talent to do well. This goes for any art form." I took it to heart, and I practice my bits in front of a mirror, to my girlfriend, to my friends, and at open mics. One of my main goals is to be good at stand-up, and it should be yours, too, because you want to have the talent when you get that big opportunity.

I've heard many comics tell me, "I want to get big." I think the aspirations of getting big in the comedy scene are great. You should always aim for greatness, and nothing lower. The problem is, you shouldn't be focused on getting big. You need to get good before anything else. For you to become big in any field, you need to have a pretty good brand for yourself. If your brand stinks, you won't get good, and for a stand-up comic, your brand, in the minds of people, needs to resonate that you are funny—so funny that they will spend however much for a ticket to see you. When you get good, your brand expands, and as it expands, you will get booked for more shows. More shows mean you get bigger. This all stems from being good. If your priority is to be big, then you are one step below the comic who is trying to get good.

In this industry, your network will help you get booked. If the comics who know you have only seen you bomb on stage, you aren't going to be the first one they offer a guest spot on their show to. Those spots are meant for people who are good, so keep in mind that you won't get a good brand if you aren't funny. Think about comics in the past who have been big, and as you think, you might find that some of those big comics aren't as big as they used to be. Their brand probably lost popularity because they did something stupid, or they weren't as good as they used to be. Even when you get back, you need to keep gathering new material—no one wants to listen to jokes they know the punchline to.

I remember, after one of my *Wicked Funny* shows, I was talking to the headliner, Usama Siddiquee, who happens to be another Bengali comedian. The difference was that he's Bangladeshi Bengali, and I am Indian Bengali. It was nice talking to another Bengali because we went through similar childhoods. We laughed about how Bengalis couldn't stop eating fish, and how loving the families are, but they're a little too loving. What I mean by that is the cheek pinching. Indians are notorious for this. As a sign of affection, Aunties would always pinch my cheeks and tell me how cute I am, but it hurt so much.

We had a good talk, and he gave me a lot of good advice about the stand-up scene. I was telling him, "Bro, I have this urge to perform, as much as I can, so I can be..." He looked at me, waiting for the end of my sentence, and I ended it with, "So I can be good." He was relieved, and told me, "Vinny, that's what you want to be. If you said, 'So I can be big,' I would have left you and walked away. That's not where you want to be. As you get good, you will be big." It was a great conversation, and I learned a lot from it. Most comics want to make it to the big leagues, and they should do whatever it takes to achieve that. They just need to have the purpose of getting good.

Throughout this whole book, I've given you many tips on what actions you should take in order to succeed. While you follow those steps, you will find yourself getting better at stand-up. Use the business strategies, which I have shared with you, as much as you can. They will help you make a name for yourself, and you won't be just any other comic but a branded one. Go over my tips related to performance and getting stage time. All of them will help you polish your stand-up, and be good. The most important thing about stand-up is you need to have fun. A comic who is having fun will have a better time doing stand-up than a comic hating every second of it and just wanting to make it at that moment. Enjoy your time at mics, and get pumped for the shows you're going to do. There was a time when I hated going to mics because I wasn't doing so well. I decided to switch my viewpoint and enjoy my time by interacting with other comics and bartenders. We would talk about funny stuff happening in our lives, and many other fun things. Because of my change in attitude, my performances started to get better. Your adventure in comedy will need you to be industrious, and it will be a lot of fun. You just need to create that fun environment for yourself.

Instead of writing a list for this chapter, I want you to tell a comedy club booker about this book. If you ever see me at a show, feel free to say hi. Also, don't be shy to ask questions about comedy because I would gladly take the time and talk to you. Bookers, who are reading this book, if you want to talk to me, just book me at your shows. My website is vpalcomedy.com. Remember, *once you go brown, you never frown.*

I usually end a stand-up performance with, "Thanks for your time! You all have been great!" This, being a book, I will have to change it a bit. I wish you the best on your journey! You are going to do great!

About the Author

Vinayak Pal was born in Houston, Texas, and was raised in Silicon Valley. He attended boarding school in Oregon, and is now in Boston, studying business and comedy at Emerson.

He performs regularly around Boston, and co-produces Emerson's *Wicked Funny Show*. *Wicked Funny* has had many professionals headline the show, who have won comedy competitions, and some who are touring internationally. Vinayak loves to perform at the Laughs Unlimited Comedy Club, in Sacramento, because the crowds there are amazing, and the venue has an amazing urban theme to it.

If you want to book Vinayak for one of your shows/events, or if you want him to speak at one of your conferences, please visit vpalcomedy.com to find out about rates and special offers.

To get more copies of this book, visit amazon.com, and type in the book's title.

The best thing to do after reading this book is pass it, or the information from it, along to others who are interested in comedy or are pursuing it. This book's purpose is to provide them with tips and steps to help them get good!

NOTES

NOTES

Comedy Is No Joke!

NOTES

Comedy Is No Joke!

NOTES

NOTES

NOTES

NOTES

Comedy Is No Joke!

NOTES

NOTES

NOTES

NOTES

NOTES

NOTES

NOTES

NOTES

Comedy Is No Joke!

NOTES

NOTES

Made in the USA
Columbia, SC
10 April 2018